THE STORY OF THE PORT OF SEATTLE

RISING TIDES AND TAILWINDS

1911 ~ 2011

Kit Oldham, Peter Blecha & The HistoryLink Staff

Project director: Tom Brown
Designer: Nancy Kinnear
Editor: Tom Brown; copy editor, Charles Smyth; indexer, Michael Billings
Townley; cover photo tinting, Emma Tupper
Published by the Port of Seattle in association with
HistoryInk / HistoryLink and University of Washington Press

University of Washington Press
PO Box 50096, Seattle, WA 98145, USA
www.washington.edu/uwpress

Printed in China
16 15 14 13 12 11 5 4 3 2 1

ISBN 978-0-295-99131-3

Library of Congress Control Number: 2011925971

The paper used in this publication meets the minimum requirements
of American National Standard for Information Sciences—Permanence of
Paper for Printed Library Materials, ANSI Z39.48-1984.∞

ABOVE: *The World Port of Seattle and Its Ocean Trade Routes*, Port of Seattle
Annual Report, 1934.

JACKET FRONT: Seattle waterfront, May 24, 1915.

TITLE PAGE: Seattle waterfront, 1874.

JACKET BACK, TOP: Gina Marie Lindsey Arrivals Hall, Seattle-Tacoma
International Airport, 2011.

BOTTOM: Terminal 46 and Seattle skyline, 2005.

CONTENTS

Foreword by Richard D. Ford 5

Introduction by Kit Oldham and Peter Blecha 6

Birth of the Port 9

Building an Institution 27

Boom and Bust 41

Into the Jet Age 55

Revolution and Recession 69

Competition and Expansion 85

Green Gateway 97

Appendix A: Port of Seattle Commissioners 115

Appendix B: Port of Seattle Directors/CEOs 116

Appendix C: Port of Seattle Union Partners 117

A Note on Sources 118

Acknowledgments 119

Image Credits 120

Index 124

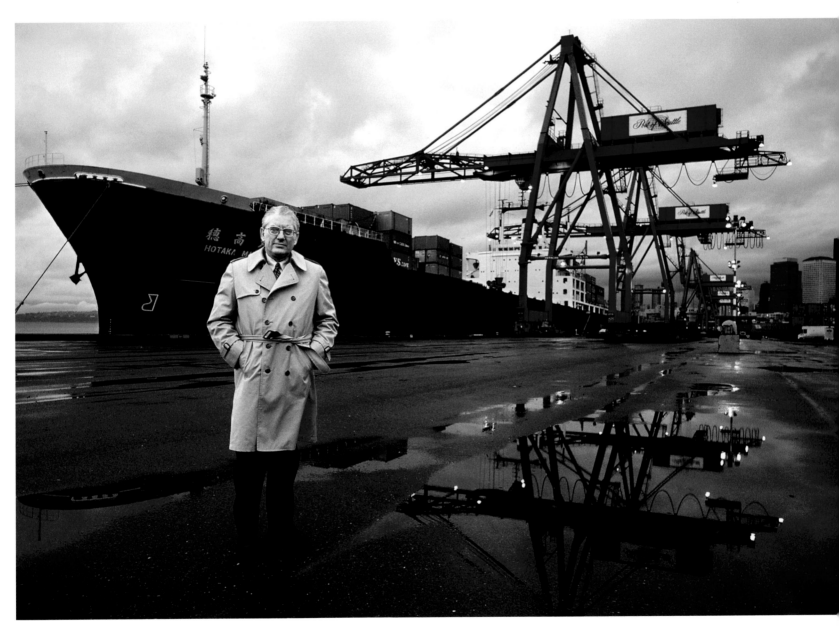

Richard Ford at Terminal 37, 1983. Ford served as Port of Seattle executive director from January 1977 through June 1985.

FOREWORD
by Richard D. Ford

If past is prologue, this 100 years of history of the Port of Seattle should help us better understand the present. The book is about dreams for the future, but also of hardships and challenges that faced each generation that served the Port.

Today's Port of Seattle each year handles more than 12 million metric tons of cargo at its seaport, serves more than 30 million passengers arriving and departing from its airport, and provides an essential home for the North Pacific fishing fleet. Today's Port seeks to fulfill the early dreams of a port that would serve as a major regional link to the world beyond the mountains to the east and across the sea to the west.

The movement that formed the Port in 1911 sought to enhance King County's economic growth and trade. To achieve their goal the citizens wanted publicly owned marine facilities to open the region to opportunities that could be reached by the sea. They understood that strong, competitive transportation was essential to economic growth.

This was more than an ideological movement; it was a movement committed to action. In 1911, voters not only approved the Port's creation, they also approved more than $3 million in general obligation bonds. That financial commitment in today's dollars would be about $70 million — and the economic value of the Port's marine terminals to today's community is several times that annually.

In 1960, while other ports debated the future of the container in ocean shipping, the Port of Seattle took the risk of building its first container terminal without a tenant until the eleventh hour as the contractors completed the project. It paid off: Seattle dominated the Pacific Northwest container business for more than a decade.

During World War II when the need for a civilian airport became critical, the Port of Seattle stepped up after others declined. The result is Seattle-Tacoma International Airport, today a premier gateway for travel and a tremendous economic contributor to our region.

Times and technology have changed drastically during the last century, but the basic vision that brought the Port of Seattle into existence remains. As a participant and an observer for half of those 100 years I have been both amazed and comforted by the Port of Seattle's pursuit of the values and mission first articulated by its founders. Looking forward, those same values and mission will provide a steady rudder in a global marketplace characterized by continuous change.

INTRODUCTION

by Kit Oldham and Peter Blecha

The history of Seattle is to a great extent the history of its waterfront. From the time of its founding by settlers who arrived by water and supported themselves selling timber to passing ships, Seattle has depended more than most cities on waterborne commerce. The city grew up where it did because of the great natural harbor of Elliott Bay, and in its first decades much of the commercial center was built literally in that harbor, on piers and fill rising over muddy tide water.

For 100 years now, Seattle's waterfront history has both shaped and been shaped by the Port of Seattle, the independent government body created in 1911 to develop public wharves, piers, waterways, and other harbor facilities essential to the region's trade-dependent economy. Much of the Port's history is visible today on Elliott Bay and beyond: tall container cranes and grain elevators bracket a downtown waterfront dotted with Port piers, parks, marinas, restaurants and conference centers, and home ports for major cruise lines and the North Pacific fishing fleet lie nearby.

While the Port was created in response to unhappiness with existing harbor conditions, its role and influence have reached far beyond the waterfront. The Port of Seattle founded, has regularly expanded and upgraded, and continues to own and operate Seattle–Tacoma International Airport. The largest airport in the Pacific Northwest, Sea-Tac

contributes more to the region, in terms of jobs and economic activity, than the Port's other efforts combined.

If the Port of Seattle did not already exist, it is hard to imagine that a government agency could be created today to own and manage the region's major airport, a leading maritime port, Fishermen's Terminal, Shilshole Bay Marina, and the many other facilities that collectively create thousands of jobs and pump billions of dollars into the regional economy. Indeed, the idea that a publicly run port should build and operate Seattle's harbor facilities was controversial a century ago. However, in 1911 progressive reformers, far-sighted civil engineers, and eventually much of the city's political and business elite joined forces to wrest revolutionized and vastly expanded Washington's international trade; and more recently has worked to address some of the region's more intractable environmental problems.

The Port has not always enjoyed smooth sailing. As this history recounts, there have been false starts, missteps, controversies, and more along the way. The Port's first commissioners faced withering criticism for policies assailed as radical, until their vision was vindicated by the Port's astounding success during World War I. Conflicts between labor and management, sometimes violent, rocked the docks for decades before more cooperative relations were forged between unions, the Port, and private employers. Similarly, intense rivalry with other ports only gradually evolved toward regional cooperation. Many challenges remain as the Port enters its second century, but Seattle and the surrounding region would be dramatically different today if not for those who created the Port of Seattle a century ago.

control of the harbor from the private railroad and shipping corporations that dominated it.

The structure that these reformers created for the Port of Seattle (and for other ports around the state) — combining public funding and governmental powers with an entrepreneurial business orientation in what scholars have dubbed "public enterprise" — proved productive and enduring. In its first century, the Port readied Seattle for the huge increase in Pacific trade that accompanied World War I; helped the area weather the Great Depression; undertook the task of building and managing Sea-Tac Airport when other agencies did not; made Seattle one of the first West Coast ports to invest in containerized shipping, which

Aerial perspective of Seattle, 1878

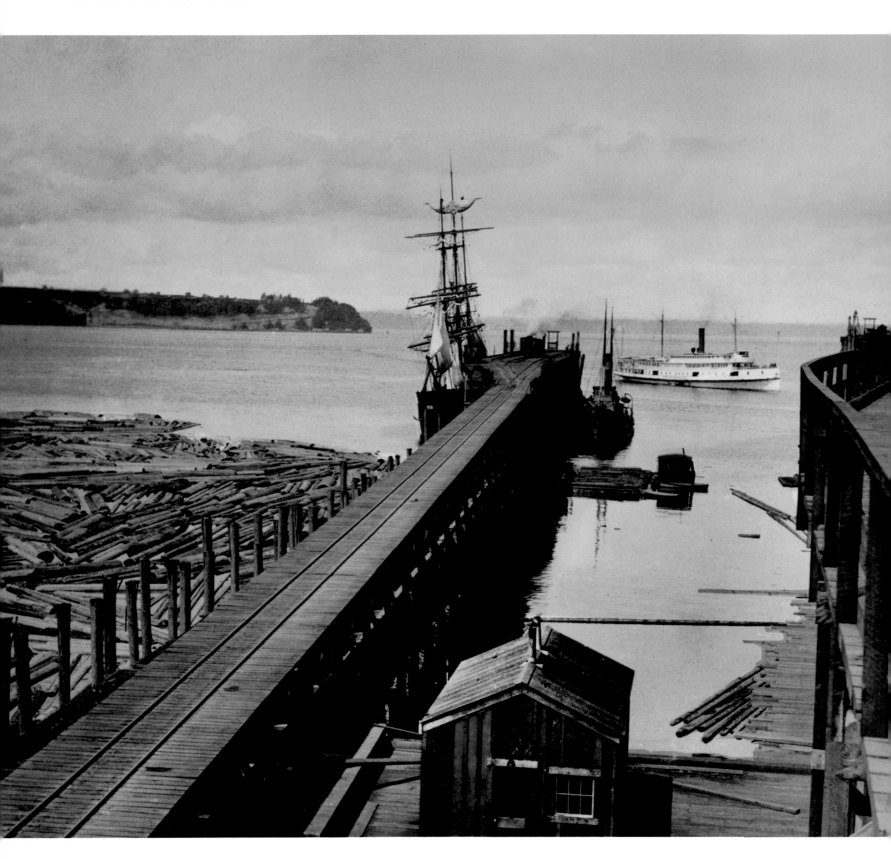

Chapter 1: **BIRTH OF THE PORT**

Water routes and railroads built Seattle. But in the early 1900s, 50 years after the city's founding, the central waterfront — the critical juncture between water and rail — was a chaotic mess. Competing private railroads dominated the waterfront, a tangle of multiple rail lines, terminals, switches, and spurs leading to a confusion of mostly small, privately owned docks, warehouses, mills, and canneries built on wooden pilings over the muddy tide flats of Elliott Bay. Front Street (today's 1st Avenue), running along the shore just inland of the high-tide line, no longer fronted the water. Three more roadways — Post Alley, Western Avenue, and Railroad Avenue (today's Alaskan Way) — paralleled Front Street to the west, running for much of their length offshore, their wood-plank surfaces raised above tide level on log pilings.

The key battleground was the aptly named Railroad Avenue, the outermost street, occupied by eight and in places nine separate lines of track that divided Seattle, physically and legally, from its all-important waterfront. From Railroad Avenue's western, waterward side, a fringe of piers and wharves reached out into the harbor. The lifeblood of the

OPPOSITE: Ships bound for Alaska or California were loaded with coal delivered by rail from mines east of Lake Washington, ca 1889.

region's economy flowed across these docks. Coal from the rich deposits south and east of Seattle, timber from Western Washington's tall forests, and grain, cotton, and machinery from across the United States arrived in rail cars to be loaded on ships bound for California or Asia, while tea, silk, rice, and other Asian imports were unloaded on the docks.

Puget Sound's famed Mosquito Fleet of small independently owned steamers also called at the Railroad Avenue piers. Along with providing the primary passenger transportation around the Sound, the fleet carried commercial goods to outlying communities and brought fresh produce from the region's farms to market in Seattle. Across Railroad Avenue from the docks, Western Avenue was lined with commission houses — warehouses where middlemen bought and resold the fresh produce that arrived daily.

However, reaching or even seeing the wharves and water from the produce warehouses and the central city beyond was not easy. Freight cars unloading or switching tracks frequently blocked views and access. Actually traversing Railroad Avenue's 150-foot width and multiple tracks by foot or horse-drawn cart was even more challenging. For pedestrians or horse teams dodging trains and bouncing over rails, the perilous journey was made worse by the often-decrepit wooden road surface. Planks were splintered or rotten, and there were more than a few "man traps" — holes through which the unwary could fall into the cesspool of rotting filth and garbage accumulated among the pilings below.

For many, Railroad Avenue's legal status was just as appalling as (and indeed a major cause of) its physical condition. Three large private corporations — the Great Northern Railway, the Northern Pacific Railroad, and the Pacific Coast Company, which mined the large coalfields in south King County and engaged in coastal trade — owned the tracks and most of the docks and warehouses that lined Railroad Avenue. This fractured private ownership posed barriers to waterfront access and trade every bit as great as the iron rails, lines of box cars, and rotten planks.

Because the railroad companies also owned the piers and warehouses, they controlled wharf availability and rates, which they arranged to serve their own interest in filling trains with cargo, rather than to promote trade and make it easier for the area's farmers and merchants to export and import goods. Beyond that, with competing track and dock owners pursuing their own separate interests, coordinated development of needed new facilities, or just improvement of existing ones, was difficult to achieve. For instance, few of the many piers were large enough to accommodate big oceangoing ships.

With the 1914 opening of the Panama Canal approaching, Seattle (like all West Coast port cities) expected a huge jump in international trade that would boost the local economy. However, city leaders saw little sign that the railroads were preparing the waterfront to meet the demands of this anticipated trade boom. As frustration grew over the railroads' legal and physical stranglehold on Seattle's waterfront, so did pressure for the formation of a publicly owned and operated port.

COURTED AND SPURNED

The problems facing the waterfront that inspired calls for a public port were rooted in both the natural history of Elliott Bay and the human history of the young city on the bay's eastern shore. Seattle was a commercial port city from its founding in 1851. In Elliott Bay, Seattle had one of the world's great deepwater ports, a large protected harbor in which even the biggest ships could anchor close to shore, as the Denny party's clothesline-and-horseshoe sounding demonstrated. But, before the massive reshaping of the land that created today's waterfront, the shore rose sharply from the water's edge with little adjacent dry flat land for commercial or industrial development. Like the Lushootseed-speaking inhabitants of

d̓id̓əlálič ("Little Place Where One Crosses Over") before them, the first settlers clustered on Piner's Point, a low spit projecting into the bay near the south end of today's downtown at Pioneer Square. From that point north, for the entire length of the present central waterfront and beyond to Smith Cove (the site of today's Terminal 91), a steep bluff covered with a tangled growth of trees rose directly from the beach.

Of necessity, therefore, Seattle's commercial waterfront, beginning with Henry Yesler's lumber mill and wharf, was built out on piers over the water. Yesler's workers dumped fill off the wharf, extending dry, level ground out into the tide flats — the muddy area left exposed at low tide but covered by up to 12 feet of water at high tide. Other landowners followed Yesler's example, using fill and pilings to create space on which to build docks, warehouses, and stores. In 1876, Front Street, the main business street running north from Yesler's Wharf, was graded and filled behind a wooden bulkhead above the beach, from which small docks stretched out into the bay. By the 1880s, new streets — Post Alley and Western Avenue — were being built beyond Front Street on fill and pilings over the tide flats.

ABOVE: Elevated railroad tracks approaching King Street coal docks, Seattle, ca. 1889.

OPPOSITE: Postcards provide early views of the Seattle waterfront.

TOP: Logs await shipment at King Street coal bunkers where vessels also refueled, 1889.

SECOND: A view of the Seattle waterfront, ca. 1907.

THIRD: Delivery wagons of the Seattle Coal and Fuel Company, Railroad Avenue S and Dearborn Street, ca. 1909.

BOTTOM: Activity along Railroad Avenue.

YESLER'S WHARF

The origins of Seattle — indeed, its very location — were based on the needs of maritime commerce. The founders of the new town were the Denny party: a couple dozen Midwestern immigrants led by Arthur Denny who had slogged their way across the Oregon Trail to Portland, and then caught Captain Robert C. Fay's schooner *Exact* up into Puget Sound — where they disembarked on November 13, 1851, at a spot along Elliott Bay that they would christen "New York, Oregon Territory." Amused by their grandiose dream, later arrivals soon humorously amended that to "New York, Alki" (a Chinook trading jargon term meaning "by-and-by" or "eventually"), and today that little dig is enshrined by West Seattle's Alki Point. Mere weeks after the Denny party's arrival, the brig *Leonesa* sailed in from San Francisco and its Captain Howard informed them that California had great need for logs to use as piles for building piers. The settlers got busy felling trees and selling them to Howard. And, with that initial transaction, the area's cargo-exporting industry commenced.

By early 1852 most of the settlers figured that their original settlement site was too exposed and blustery and they sought out a better one. Borrowing a canoe from the local *dxʷdəwʔábš* ("People of the Inside," or "Duwamish") natives, Denny and a few other men, using Mary Denny's 100-foot clothesline with a horseshoe as a sounding lead, set out to plumb the depths of the bay. Pleased to discover that the horseshoe never touched bottom — it was as deep as 200 feet just a few yards off the east bank of the bay — they climbed up the bank near a spot a few blocks south of today's Yesler Way, originally mapped as "Piner's Point" by the Wilkes Expedition in 1841. It was the site of a Duwamish village named *dᶻidᶻəlálič* ("Little Place Where One Crosses Over"), a trailhead from Elliot Bay to points east.

On February 15th they returned to stake claims and soon began constructing log cabins. In April the first group of the Denny party began moving over from New York, Alki. Initially they dubbed their new outpost "Duwamps," but by the summer of 1853 — and as their friendship with the main local chief, *siʔał* (1780-1866), deepened — the settlers renamed it with the anglicized version of his name: Seattle. In late 1852 Henry Yesler arrived and announced his intention to build a steam-powered sawmill somewhere on the sound. He was encouraged to stay with the gift of a strip of land (which became known as Mill Street — today's Yesler Way) that had direct waterfront access. That winter the construction of a wharf, mill, and cookhouse (from hand-squared logs) began and by March 1853 — the same month that Washington Territory was officially split off from Oregon Territory — Yesler's Mill, the village's first industry, was operational. The mill and its little wharf became the hub of the nascent town's economy, providing employment to both settlers and Native Americans. Yesler's Wharf grew in length after he hired local Indians to help extend its base by dumping rocks and debris off its end. Those laborers also sealed the fate of their own, once-bountiful flounder grounds in the tidal pool behind *dᶻidᶻəlálič* by filling it in with mill sawdust and trimmings.

When Thomas Mercer arrived in October 1853 with the town's first two horses and a wagon, he pioneered Seattle's first "intermodal" connections by carting goods to and from ships docked at the wharf. Yesler's Wharf played a key role in much of the young town's early life: it was where a navy sloop-of-war, the USS *Decatur*, docked during the Indian War of 1856, and later became home to Puget Sound's legendary Mosquito Fleet passenger service. By the late 1860s the wharf had grown to a 200-foot length, and it expanded to an impressive 1,000 feet the following decade. Like much of pioneer Seattle, Yesler's old mill and wharf were destroyed in the Great Fire of 1889.

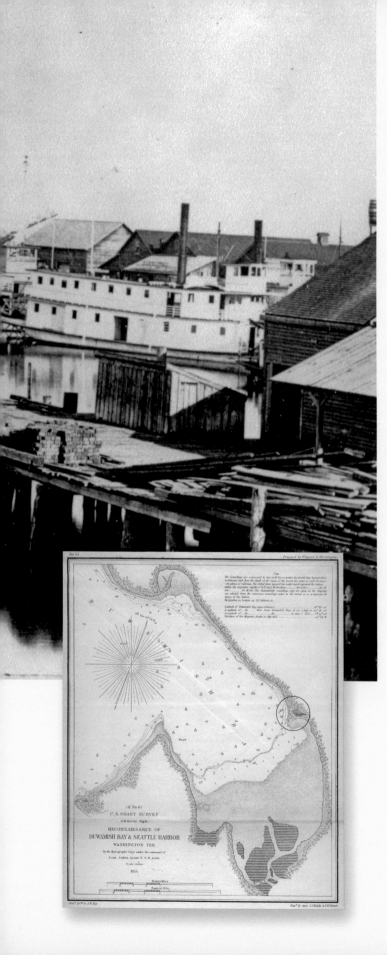

CENTER: Yesler's Wharf is stacked with lumber shipments while Mosquito Fleet vessels are moored at the adjacent dock.

ABOVE TOP: Old-growth trees like these gave truth to the legends of Northwest bounty and provided much of the region's early exports.

ABOVE: In the early 1900s, lumber mills dotted Puget Sound from Samish Bay to Olympia.

MAP: The Duwamish estuary and Seattle harbor as they existed in 1854, with circle indicating the Seattle settlement area and approximate location of Yesler's Wharf.

When railroad tracks reached Seattle in the 1870s, they too were built on piers and trestles extending well out into the water. This was due in part to physical necessity, but the many railroad trestles also reflected the history of Seattle's off-and-on courtship of and by transcontinental railroad lines. Seattle residents, like those of virtually every settlement in Washington Territory, hoped and expected that their home would become the terminus of a transcontinental railroad and therefore the commercial and population center of the region. But in 1873, the Northern Pacific, the first transcontinental line to reach the Northwest, spurned Seattle, choosing the upstart town of Tacoma, 30 miles south on Puget Sound, as its western terminus. Seattle leaders had offered the railroad 7,500 lots, 3,000 additional acres, and $250,000 in cash and bonds, but they could not compete with Tacoma's grant of its entire townsite on the west side of Commencement Bay, which gave the NP a nearly complete real estate monopoly around the new terminus.

Seattle was able to prosper despite this slight because its existing development, excellent harbor, and central position on Puget Sound made it the logical home port for the Mosquito Fleet of small steamships, and thus the center of regional commerce in lumber, coal, produce, manufactured goods, and other cargo. Still, Seattle civic leaders wanted a railroad and, with none in sight, decided to build their own. The local line never made it farther east than the coalfields of Renton and Newcastle, but it did set a precedent: Its tracks reached King Street from the south via a trestle across the tidelands, which at that time reached east all the way to the foot of Beacon Hill.

Several years later, the local owners sold their railroad to Henry Villard, who raised the city's hopes when he acquired control of the Northern Pacific in 1881 and promised to bring the transcontinental line to Seattle. In return, Villard requested a right-of-way along the central waterfront, which the city happily granted. Villard brought the promised branch line to Seattle, but when he lost control of the Northern Pacific in 1884, new management all but abandoned the Seattle link in favor of Tacoma.

In response, a new railroad effort was led by Judge Thomas Burke, a lawyer and real estate speculator who was one of Seattle's wealthiest and most influential citizens — and whose wishes were rarely refused by judges and other local elected officials. In 1885, Burke organized a local railroad with Daniel Gilman and other partners (the line's route along lakes Union and Washington is now the popular Burke-Gilman Trail).

It was Burke who conceived Railroad Avenue. In order to outflank the Northern Pacific, which controlled the existing right-of-way along the waterfront, Burke prevailed on a sympathetic city council to dedicate a new 120-foot-wide "street" (it would later expand) over the tidewater beyond the existing waterfront, and grant his line a 30-foot right-of-way along this street. This action was legally questionable because, while Washington was a territory, the federal government held title to all tidelands. But there was ample precedent for private use of tidelands in the many docks and buildings constructed on pilings and the earlier railroad rights of way.

Railroad Avenue began taking physical shape in April 1887, when the first of 26,000 piles, cut in nearby forests, were driven into the Elliott Bay muck. The first trestle, then just one track wide, was finished later that year. In 1889, Seattle's great fire destroyed part of this original Railroad Avenue, although a bucket brigade saved some northern portions. Railroad Avenue was one of the first things rebuilt after the fire, and it was broadened and extended, as were Western Avenue and Post Alley lying between it and dry land.

In 1890, Burke's Railroad Avenue right-of-way fell into the hands of the Northern Pacific, but by then the company had curtailed its efforts to quash Seattle. Well on its way to becoming the leading metropolis of Puget Sound, Seattle was now being wooed by another transcontinental line, James J. Hill's Great Northern Railway. Hill, a visionary railroad mogul based in Minnesota, was pushing his line across the northernmost tier of the United States to Puget Sound, which he saw as a jumping-off point for trade with China, Japan, and other Asian countries.

Seattle's location, harbor, and commercial development made it a logical place for the Great Northern's terminus, and Hill had the good sense to engage the persuasive and influential Thomas Burke as his local agent. Having previously achieved the creation of

ABOVE LEFT: James Hill, center, controlled the Great Northern Railway and the Northern Pacific Railroad, which eventually merged and now are incorporated in the Burlington Northern Santa Fe Railway.

ABOVE RIGHT: Thomas Burke built his law career in Seattle. The Burke-Gilman trail and Burke Museum are named for him.

OPPOSITE ABOVE: The Great Seattle Fire of 1889 as seen from the waterfront. The fire burned the entire business district, four of the city's wharves, and its railroad terminals.

BELOW: Columbia & Puget Sound Railroad station and docks, ca. 1882.

ABOVE TOP AND ABOVE: Passengers pack onto the vessel *Victoria*, ca. 1904-1910.

ABOVE RIGHT: Alaska Steamship Company brochure.

Railroad Avenue, Burke had little difficulty persuading the city council — over the vociferous objections of the Northern Pacific — to give Hill and the Great Northern a 60-foot right-of-way down the middle of the wood-planked roadway.

The Great Northern reached Seattle in 1893, and by 1895 there were four transcontinental rail lines jostling for position on the waterfront. Seattle finally had its continental connections and a rapidly burgeoning international trade. Japan's Nippon Yusen Kaisha shipping line contracted with the Great Northern in 1896 to begin regular steamship service between Seattle and Japan. Hill soon launched his own ocean liners, the *Minnesota* and the *Dakota*. Dubbed the "largest cargo carriers afloat," they carried passengers and goods from Smith Cove to China, Japan, and the Philippines.

Moreover, because the city already dominated trade with Alaska, it was to Seattle's harbor that the steamer *Portland* sailed in 1897 with the fabled "ton of gold" that ignited the Klondike Gold Rush. Seattle became the primary jumping-off point for the swarms of gold seekers hurrying to Alaska and Canada in search of instant wealth, boosting the city's economy and population to new highs. The gold rush put Seattle on the national map as the gateway to the Klondike and Yukon goldfields. It also pumped money into local businesses, as the hordes of would-be millionaires who were heading north and the few who had struck it rich and were heading home spent much of their money in the city. The influx of capital and the demand for services helped boost steel, lumber, and other industries in the region, spurred the growth of roads, water and sewer systems, and other infrastructure, and boosted shipbuilding and waterfront commerce. In the first few years of the 1900s, private rail and dock owners built new wharves and terminals along the waterfront at a rapid pace. But despite the economic benefits, this uncoordinated development did not improve, and in some cases exacerbated, the tangled and dangerous mess that Railroad Avenue and the central waterfront had become.

A BLOT ON THE CITY

Well before it had reached that stage, some voices were proposing a different vision for the waterfront. As early as 1890, prominent engineer and municipal planner Virgil G. Bogue argued that all harbors in the state should be publicly owned. Bogue, who would go on to draft grandiose development plans for Seattle and other Washington cities and ports, had spent his early career working for the railroads, but he did not hesitate to criticize how they were using Seattle's great natural harbor. In an 1895 proposal for coordinated waterfront development, Bogue described the existing condition of Railroad Avenue, separating downtown and the docks "with trains frequently passing, switching going on, and cars and trains standing on the various tracks," as "an exceptional state of affairs scarcely equaled elsewhere" and "a blot on the city and a menace to the lives of its people."

Vessels of Puget Sound's Mosquito Fleet take every foot of space at Colman Dock.

MOSQUITO FLEET

For decades after settlers began trickling into the Puget Sound region, the main mode of transportation between new port towns like Tumwater, Seattle, Tacoma, Port Townsend, and Bellingham was via watercraft. Without horse paths, wagon roads, or railroads those newcomers — like the indigenous inhabitants all around them — took to paddling dugout canoes to travel, and then began importing or building boats and ships. In 1852, Bob Moxlie's Olympia-based "canoe express" service began making regular U.S. mail deliveries to Seattle, and in 1853 regular ferry service around Puget Sound began at Henry Yesler's wharf with the Gove brothers' side-wheeler steamship *Fairy*.

By 1865, a swarm of independently operated small steamers, which due to their sheer numbers, buzzing engines, and maneuverability came to be called the Mosquito Fleet, greatly increased passenger service to the growing number of farming communities, logging camps, and mills on Puget Sound and up the Duwamish, Snohomish, Skagit, and other rivers, adding to the hustle and bustle on Seattle's waterfront. It was largely due to the efficiency of the Mosquito Fleet, whose routes radiated around the sound from Seattle, that the Northern Pacific Railroad's 1873 decision to locate its transcontinental terminus in Tacoma wasn't a death knell for Seattle. Indeed, future banker and then-steamship operator Joshua Green later recalled: "These small Puget Sound steamer lines kept our merchants in close daily touch with all of Puget Sound in the '80's and '90's."

The Mosquito Fleet played a significant role in Seattle commerce well into the twentieth century and figured prominently in the passage of the Port District Act and the early growth of the Port of Seattle. Legislators and voters from small towns around the sound supported the act, and eventually created port districts of their own, largely to supply better facilities for the Mosquito Fleet steamers that connected them to Seattle and the rest of the world. Even at the Port of Seattle, where the first commissioners prepared the harbor for an expansion of international trade, serving the local Mosquito Fleet was a high priority.

The primary objective of the Bell Street Terminal, one of the Port's first projects, was to provide adequate docking space for Mosquito Fleet steamers, which were then at the mercy of crowded, privately owned docks that favored the big shipping lines. An early Port publication noted the importance of the fleet to Seattle's commerce, stating "these 'mosquito boat' lines are equivalent to branch railway lines radiating from the Seattle waterfront," making Seattle the distribution point for goods bound to "the myriad towns and settlements among the outspread fingers of Puget Sound." On their return to Seattle, the boats carried fresh produce and other products to the Bell Street Terminal, with its ample new cold storage space and a viaduct over Railroad Avenue giving easy access to nearby Pike Place Market, "enabling producers of berries, eggs, vegetables, poultry and fish from neighboring islands and across-Sound points to reach Seattle buyers through the public market."

Throughout the Port's first two decades Mosquito Fleet shipping remained an important part of its operations. Not until the late 1920s and 1930s did automobiles and highways supplant the waterborne transportation system, with diesel auto ferries replacing passenger steamers on the few remaining water routes.

Topping the hill on the right, the Denny Hotel
dominates this view of the Seattle waterfront and
northern downtown. The hotel, located on 3rd
Avenue between Stewart and Virginia, was razed
in 1906.

ABOVE: This view of Railroad Avenue looking north shows the treacherous path pedestrians crossed to reach the waterfront.

OPPOSITE ABOVE: Reginald Thomson
CENTER: George Cotterill
BELOW: Robert Bridges

Bogue was part of a national Progressive movement, particularly strong in Washington, that advocated public control of essential services. Reformers worked on many fronts, and there were long struggles for greater regulation of the railroads and for municipal ownership of water and electric utilities (Seattle would become one of the first cities in the country to create city water and electric departments). In Washington, with its many port cities and strong dependence on trade, the battle for public control of the waterfront was especially contentious.

Disposition of the tidelands, which the federal government turned over to the new state upon Washington's admission to the Union, was among the most controversial issues when the state constitution was drafted in 1889. The railroads, shipping companies, merchants, and others who had built up their businesses on the tidelands insisted that they should receive legal title to the land they occupied. But Eastern Washington farmers, whose ability to export crops was limited by the railroad stranglehold on tracks and docks, joined urban reformers in support of state ownership. In the end, the constitutional convention compromised. The new constitution declared the state owned the tidelands but authorized the Washington Legislature to lease that land to private interests. It also set up a commission empowered to establish public harbor areas for incorporated cities.

To the surprise of many, the first state Harbor Lines Commission, created in 1890 with a three-year term, heeded Bogue and others who believed the entire harbor should be public. It designated a large public harbor area for Seattle, encompassing all of Railroad Avenue and much of the Elliott Bay waterfront. On behalf of the railroads, Thomas Burke immediately initiated a string of lawsuits challenging the commission's decision. Although the courts ultimately rejected Burke's arguments, he achieved his goal: The litigation dragged on until after the commission's term expired, preventing implementation of its harbor plan. Several years later, a new commission drew harbor lines for Seattle that carefully left all the existing waterfront facilities in private hands.

Although the railroads had prevailed, efforts for public, or at least coordinated, harbor development continued. In 1895, working for the King County Board of Tideland Appraisers, Bogue presented the waterfront plan in which he denounced conditions on Railroad Avenue. Citing successful ports elsewhere (he named Venice, Glasgow, and New York), the engineer asserted that "the greatest commercial success has resulted where there has been, either in part or in whole, municipal or other public ownership and control of dock frontage." In his plan, Bogue proposed a single terminal company to control and coordinate waterfront facilities. Bogue won the agreement of some rail lines, but opposition from the Great Northern doomed the plan. Nevertheless, the contrast between the efficient new port envisioned by Bogue and the existing waterfront chaos helped convince more Seattle leaders that a public body was needed to modernize the waterfront.

The Panic of 1893, a nationwide depression and the first of a series of economic downturns to hit Washington in its first 20 years of statehood, boosted reform movements. Three years later, reformers briefly banded together in the short-lived Populist Party to capture the state legislature and the governor's mansion. The party fell apart before accomplishing much, but the state lands commissioner it elected, Robert Bridges, went on to play a critical role as one of the Port of Seattle's first commissioners.

After the Populist Party imploded, the reform banner was picked up by the Progressives, who operated mostly within the existing Republican and Democratic parties. Progressives tended to be educated urban professionals. Along with municipal ownership, they advocated an array of reforms, supporting labor rights, women's suffrage, and prohibition. In turn, both unions and women's suffrage organizations were strong backers of municipal ownership. Not surprisingly, the longshoremen who worked the docks were especially interested in promoting public control of waterfront areas, both to create more shipping and therefore jobs and to provide a counterweight to the strength of private employers.

In Seattle, civil engineers were among the leading Progressives. Along with Bogue, there were City Engineer Reginald H. Thomson, who built Seattle's Cedar River water and power systems and leveled various in-town hills in massive regrading projects, and George F. Cotterill, Thomson's one-time assistant who went on to draft legislation creating public ports and to serve four terms on the Seattle Port Commission.

The strong-willed and politically astute Thomson argued successfully against James J. Hill's proposal for a massive Great Northern terminal on the central waterfront. Thomson foresaw that it would interfere with creating new industrial land south of downtown on the tidelands near the mouth of the Duwamish River (land that ultimately would become a major part of the Port of Seattle) and eventually persuaded Hill to bring the Great Northern tracks under downtown in a tunnel. The tunnel (still used today) did not eliminate waterfront congestion but helped keep it from worsening.

Meanwhile, Thomson and Cotterill took another small step toward coordinating waterfront development in 1897, when they persuaded the railroads and other waterfront owners to accept a new alignment of the piers that projected out from Railroad Avenue. Until then, all piers were built at right angles to the street, but since the street, following the line of the bay, turned several times, docks on different sides of the harbor pointed at each other and, if built far enough out, would collide. The engineers proposed instead that all new piers be built on an east-west alignment. Along the central waterfront, where the shore and streets run southeast to northwest, this had the added advantage of allowing trains and ships to pull up to docks and slips without making sharp turns. The flurry of

ABOVE TOP: General Hiram Chittenden of the U.S. Army Corps of Engineers not only directed construction of the Lake Washington Ship Canal and the locks in Ballard but was known for improvements at Yellowstone (where he laid out the road network) and Yosemite national parks.

ABOVE RIGHT: The Government Locks in Ballard, later renamed for Hiram Chittenden, opened navigation from Lake Washington to Puget Sound in 1917.

ABOVE: The opening of the Panama Canal in 1914 raised hopes for increased waterborne trade.

wharf-building that followed the 1897 Klondike Gold Rush, although otherwise uncoordinated, conformed to this new alignment, as has subsequent development.

CREATING THE PORT

Cotterill combined engineering work with political activity. In 1907, as chairman of the state Senate Committee on Harbors and Harbor Lines, he drafted the first bill to authorize public ports in Washington, which would have created port districts with limited powers. In addition to those calling for public control of Seattle's harbor, the bill won support from many around the state who believed public port facilities could benefit their communities. These backers included farmers and merchants in small Puget Sound towns who wanted better docks to attract Mosquito Fleet service; longshoremen's locals from Seattle and Tacoma; and businessmen from Hoquiam and other port cities, who, like their Seattle counterparts, wanted to prepare for the expected trade boom when the Panama Canal opened. However, Governor Albert E. Mead vetoed the 1907 bill, and proposed legislation failed again in 1909, blocked by railroad interests and mill owners.

By the end of the decade, railroad obstruction of public harbor improvements in Seattle was driving even conservative business leaders and politicians, along with the city's two major newspapers, the *Seattle Post-Intelligencer* and *The Seattle Times* — all generally opposed to municipal ownership — to support the concept of a public port. Two long-anticipated canal projects, one local and one international, played central roles in the growing consensus that Seattle needed a public port authority.

Locally, almost from the time the city was founded, Seattleites dreamed of a canal connecting Elliott Bay to Lake Washington, the large freshwater lake on the city's eastern side, but disagreed on where to locate it. Some favored linking the existing waterways of Portage Bay, Lake Union, and Salmon Bay — the northern route on which the ship canal was finally built. Others promoted a southern route that was more direct but required cutting through the 375-foot-high ridge of Beacon Hill. The northern canal prevailed after General Hiram M. Chittenden, yet another dynamic and progressive civil engineer who would leave his mark on the city and Port of Seattle, took charge of the federal Army

GEORGE F. COTTERILL

George F. Cotterill proposed Washington's first port district legislation, cowrote the Port District Act, and served 12 years as a Port of Seattle commissioner. Yet the Port was just one aspect of his long and varied career. A lifelong teetotaler and ardent prohibitionist, a civil engineer by training and a social engineer by temperament, and a perennial (but rarely successful) political candidate, he held many positions and championed a wide range of progressive reforms with varying degrees of success.

Cotterill was born in England in 1865 and moved with his family to New Jersey when he was 6. His parents pledged abstinence from alcohol and were deeply involved in the temperance movement. Cotterill inherited their zeal and for his entire life prohibition was his most passionate cause.

Graduating from high school as valedictorian at 15, Cotterill considered studying law at Yale, but instead went to work for a local civil engineer who taught him surveying and civil engineering. At 19, Cotterill moved to Seattle and did survey work for mines, railroads, and other projects. Eventually he went to work for surveyor and engineer for R. H. Thomson and when Thomson became Seattle city engineer Cotterill joined him as assistant city engineer. They collaborated on numerous projects, from building sewers and bicycle trails to filling tide flats and replatting the waterfront.

One of their most important achievements was developing the city's publicly owned Cedar River water system. Both men were staunch advocates of publicly controlled utilities, but Seattle lacked money to construct the Cedar River system. Cotterill seized on a novel funding scheme whereby the city would issue construction bonds to be repaid from the anticipated water revenues. The arrangement that allowed Seattle to build its public water system became a standard financing method for public utilities across the country.

Appalled by Seattle's "open city" policy that tolerated gambling, prostitution, and other vices, Cotterill ran unsuccessfully for mayor in 1900. For the next two decades he sought some office in almost every election, winning twice. He served one term in the state Senate (1907-1910) and one contentious term (1912-1914) as mayor of Seattle.

A Democrat in an era when Republicans dominated state politics, Cotterill frequently worked with like-minded Republicans under the Populist and Progressive banners. He achieved some of his greatest political success as a leader in the Progressive-dominated legislative sessions of 1907 and 1909. Along with the Port District Act (not finally enacted until after he lost his Senate seat), he helped win legislative approval for the state constitutional amendment, subsequently approved by voters, that granted women the right to vote.

During his tenure on the Port of Seattle Commission beginning in 1922, Cotterill went along with fellow commissioners George Lamping and W. S. Lincoln as they moved the formerly radical Port in the direction of the city's conservative establishment. He also pushed for tighter control of the waterfront to eliminate illegal liquor shipments — Mayor Edwin "Doc" Brown, no fan of Prohibition or prohibitionists, responded by presenting Cotterill with a corkscrew purportedly representing the public mood.

Cotterill was nearing 60 when he lost his commission seat. He eventually retired from a position in the King County assessor's office at age 84. Cotterill was 92 when he died in 1958.

Railroad Avenue in 1911.

Corps of Engineers Seattle district office in 1906 and endorsed that route. Congress soon provided funding for the locks that would be necessary (and that were eventually named in honor of Chittenden), on the condition that local funds pay for the canal itself.

In addition to building their own canal, Seattle civic leaders wanted to ready the harbor for the opening of the Panama Canal, which they (and their counterparts in cities up and down the West Coast) anticipated would bring large increases in waterborne trade with the eastern seaboard and Europe. Because the shorter water route through the canal would not increase train cargo (indeed, it meant competition for the transcontinental lines), the rail corporations that owned Seattle's waterfront had little incentive to prepare for more intercoastal shipping. Seattle leaders feared the city would fall behind rival western ports — Los Angeles, San Francisco, Portland — that were already investing in docks and wharves to attract the expected new shipping. Even nearby Tacoma, which had long lagged behind its neighbor in maritime trade, was catching up, and in 1910 began building Washington's first municipally owned dock. *The Seattle Times*, usually allergic to any whiff of municipal ownership, editorialized that Seattle should follow suit and "determine this question of city-owned docks in the affirmative." With railroads in control of the central waterfront, proponents of new facilities looked to the undeveloped land along the Duwamish River.

In 1909, the legislature, even as it rejected public port legislation, authorized King County voters to establish separate local improvement districts that could issue bonds and levy taxes to build the Lake Washington Ship Canal and develop the lower Duwamish into a waterway for large oceangoing ships. The King County commissioners approved a combined $1.75 million bond issue for the two projects, and two future port commissioners — Robert Bridges, the Populist firebrand, and Charles E. Remsberg, a Fremont banker, attorney, and real estate speculator — headed the campaign for the bond issue, which won easily in the November 1910 election.

Railroad attorneys immediately sued to invalidate the local improvement districts and managed to block work on the Duwamish Waterway for a time, but this latest attempt to obstruct projects that much of Seattle's commercial and business establishment considered essential was the last straw. When the 1911 legislative session opened, a broad consensus favored creating public port districts in Washington. Said Governor Marion E. Hay: "The people of this state are in favor of public docks and wharves and such harbor improvements as will aid commerce and navigation for the benefit of all."

The legislature passed the Port District Act, which Governor Hay signed into law on March 14, 1911. The act was drafted by Cotterill, Thomson, and Seattle Corporation Counsel Scott Calhoun, a young lawyer active in the Seattle Commercial Club, one of the civic organizations pushing for a public port. The Port District Act authorized the voters of any county in Washington to create a port district to acquire, construct, and operate waterways, docks, wharves, and other harbor improvements; rail and water transfer and terminal facilities; and ferry systems. The inclusion of ferry systems reflected frustration in King County and elsewhere with private ferry operators. A port district would be a governmental body, independent of any existing county, city, or other government, with the power to levy taxes and issue bonds, run by three elected commissioners serving without compensation. Port districts were given additional broad powers, including authority to acquire property by eminent domain, to set wharf and dock rates, and to lease port-owned property to private operators.

Even before the Port District Act took effect on June 8, 1911, Calhoun and the Commercial Club organized an ad hoc committee, with representatives from the Seattle Chamber of Commerce, Municipal League, Rotary Club, Manufacturers' Association, and other groups, to form a port district in King County. As soon as the act was law, the committee quickly collected the signatures needed to place creation of the Port of Seattle on the county's September 5 ballot.

Recognizing that a public port would be of little use if the railroads and private dock owners dominated the Port Commission, Calhoun's committee also screened potential candidates for the three commissioner positions, endorsing three at a July 28 meeting. For the central district, the committee selected Hiram Chittenden, the well-respected former Army Corps of Engineers officer. The committee's choice for the south district was the combative former state Lands Commissioner Robert Bridges, controversial for his radical views but a tireless advocate for the Duwamish waterway district. Charles Remsberg, the Republican banker from Fremont chosen for the north district, was supposed to balance the Populist Bridges on the ticket, but he was as committed to municipal ownership as his fellow nominees and in some respects proved as radical as Bridges.

With support from the press, civic organizations, politicians, and most of the business community, the proposition to create the Port of Seattle passed on September 5, 1911, by a wide margin, 13,771 votes to 4,538. Chittenden more than doubled his opponent's votes, while Bridges and Remsberg won by lesser but still substantial margins.

The Port of Seattle was a reality, but the broad-based support that led to its creation quickly evaporated, enveloping the new commissioners in controversy almost as soon as they took office.

The area around Pike Place Market hums with activity, ca. 1907.

Chapter 2: **BUILDING AN INSTITUTION**

Controversy arose soon after the newly elected Port commissioners settled down to prepare a "comprehensive scheme of harbor improvement," as required by the Port District Act. Their plan included a large, deep-sea pier and terminal at Smith Cove, another large pier and slip on the East Waterway, a small public dock, wharf, and warehouse on the central waterfront, additional general moorage on Salmon Bay (the plan was soon modified to build Fishermen's Terminal at Salmon Bay), and new ferry service on Lake Washington.

Of necessity, these projects were planned on largely undeveloped land near the fringes of the developed waterfront. East Waterway, still in its infancy, was the portion of the dredged Duwamish channel lying between the mainland south of downtown and artificial Harbor Island. Smith Cove, site of the Great Northern terminal and piers, was north of downtown in the Interbay area between Queen Anne and Magnolia hills, while Salmon Bay marked the northern end of Interbay. Even the central waterfront terminal, which would serve the Mosquito Fleet and house the Port's headquarters for many years, was located at the foot of Bell Street, then well north of the core business district.

OPPOSITE: Men stand above the hold of a ship on Seattle's waterfront as cargo is loaded, ca. 1920s.

Harbor Island in 1912. Looking Across the Bay Toward the Business Section of Seattle.

Photo by Nowell & Rognon, Seattle.

The new Plans for the development of Harbor Island and the East Waterway, Seattle, U.S.A.

But even as the commission prepared its plans, much of the downtown business establishment, headed by the Chamber of Commerce and vociferously represented by *The Seattle Times* and the *Seattle Post-Intelligencer*, promoted a very different view of the Port's proper role. Predictably, the railroads and private dock owners viewed the proposed public docks as unwanted competition. The press and other downtown businesses, which as a last resort had supported a public port to overcome the railroad monopoly on the waterfront, abhorred the idea of a public body operating commercial facilities like docks and wharves. They argued that the purpose of a public port was to use the powers of taxation, bonding, and condemnation to acquire land and fund comprehensive port improvements that private owners would not or could not undertake, but then to turn construction and operation of those facilities over to private enterprise.

And the Chamber, *Times*, and *P-I* had in mind a particular plan which fit that description: erection of a "Bush Terminal on Harbor Island." The idea of replicating the huge New York City terminal, famous as the largest and most modern in the nation, on the recently created and still-undeveloped island at the mouth of the Duwamish, first appeared in a comprehensive plan for the City of Seattle proposed in 1911 by Virgil Bogue. In that ambitious and costly proposal, Bogue, who had earlier prepared the 1895 waterfront plan torpedoed by the Great Northern, called for an ornate new Civic Center in the Denny Regrade, many new boulevards and parks, and extensive harbor improvements, including seven enormous piers and terminals on Harbor Island modeled on New York's Bush Terminals.

The press and downtown businesses strongly opposed most of Bogue's plan (contributing to its overwhelming defeat at the polls), but embraced the idea that a massive "Bush Terminal" type of complex would prepare Seattle for the trade that they expected to flow from the opening of the Panama Canal in 1914. Largely unstated but equally important to much of the business community was that if the Port confined itself to the Harbor Island plan, it would not own and operate other docks in competition with private enterprise.

That the Bush Terminal Company itself had little or no interest in building on Harbor Island did not deter the Seattle businessmen supporting the proposal, who recruited R. F. Ayers, a Bush advertising executive who left his job to promote the plan. The coalition pushing the Harbor Island plan also had the active support of Scott Calhoun, though his involvement was questionable, since the young lawyer who had helped draft and lobby for passage of the Port District Act was now serving as the Port's chief legal counsel. Calhoun traveled to New York City and returned in January 1912 with a "gentlemen's agreement" committing the Port to provide $5 million in bond money for the Harbor Island terminals — in direct violation of instructions from Port Commission President Hiram Chittenden that he was not authorized to bind the Port.

All three commissioners considered the plan deeply flawed. Not only did it place the risk on the Port while giving the profit to the private investors, but it was also an "absolute extravagance," unnecessarily large enough to accommodate not just all

Seattle's existing trade but all that from Puget Sound, Portland, Grays Harbor, Victoria, and Vancouver, B.C., as well. Moreover, as Chittenden explained, beginning the Port's development on Harbor Island did not make engineering sense. The island did not yet have any connections to shore ("Bush Terminal" supporters wanted the Port to build a tunnel or bridge), whereas the also-undeveloped East Waterway was immediately adjacent to downtown and would provide much better shipping connections. Chittenden wrote:

> It [the East Waterway development] will stay as long as Seattle lasts and its importance will grow with the growth of the city. As business develops it will expand down the waterway and along the Harbor Island front which, by that time we may hope, will have better connection with the mainland. In due time, the north shore of Harbor Island will come to its own, but to go there now is simply to force an unnatural growth.

Despite this explanation, which accurately forecast the Port's eventual development, Chittenden reluctantly agreed to add $5 million for Harbor Island to the $3 million in bonds the commission was proposing for its other projects. But he wrote the proposition such that the money would go to Ayers' Pacific Terminal Company only if it posted a performance bond to guarantee its obligations. Remsberg followed Chittenden's lead, while Robert Bridges adamantly opposed the Harbor Island plan, leading to calls for his resignation.

On March 5, 1912, King County voters approved all eight port measures on the ballot. The Port's comprehensive plan won overwhelmingly, as did bond issues for work at Smith Cove, the East Waterway, Salmon Bay, and the central waterfront, and creation of a Lake Washington ferry. The Harbor Island bonds also passed, but by narrower margins.

ABOVE LEFT: The Port's Bell Street Pier Rooftop Park, which opened in 1915.

ABOVE RIGHT: The Bell Street Pier in 1915 incorporated a wharf, a marine terminal with warehouse, cold storage, and the original Port of Seattle headquarters.

OPPOSITE TOP: Workers stack bales of hemp from India in a warehouse, ca. 1926.

CENTER: Harbor Island as it appeared in a 1912 postcard.

BELOW: Postcard vision of proposed Harbor Island development, ca. 1912.

Parallel piers improved navigation for ships and reduced waterfront chaos. This is the view west down Yesler Way, ca. 1913.

Debate over the Harbor Island proposal continued for 15 months after the bonds were approved. In August, the Port entered a contract with the Pacific Terminal Company, but it was not carried out. Ayers and his allies never managed to raise the required $310,000 in performance bonds, and in April 1913 the commissioners terminated the contract. Then, on June 17, voters agreed to the Port's request to cancel the Harbor Island bonds and substitute a $3 million bond for East Waterway work instead. Although the press bitterly blamed the commission for the failure of the Harbor Island Terminal scheme, voters also soundly rejected a proposal backed by the Chamber of Commerce and the *P-I* (the *Times* remained neutral) to add two new commission members in an effort to undermine the power of the existing commissioners.

RADICAL GROWTH

As the Harbor Island controversy was playing out, the Port Commission proceeded with its own projects. Soon after the initial March 1912 vote, the commission began its first condemnation proceeding to acquire land at Smith Cove, where the Port would build the largest pier on the West Coast, a half-mile long and a city-block wide, for loading coal, lumber, and other bulk shipments. The court action was necessary because the Great Northern Railway, which owned the land, refused to sell.

The Port awarded its first construction contracts in November 1912, for work at Salmon Bay and on the East Waterway. On Salmon Bay, the commissioners planned a home for the large Puget Sound fishing fleet. At the time, the several hundred purse seiners, gillnetters, and other fishing vessels were scattered in anchorages around Puget Sound, with no central point for provisioning and repairs. The "snug harbor" on Salmon Bay (as it was dubbed in the Port's 1912 annual report) became Fishermen's Terminal, which for nearly a century has been home to the North Pacific fishing fleet and a major economic driver for the region.

It was at the future Fishermen's Terminal, on February 15, 1913, that the first construction in Port of Seattle history began, with workers driving the first piles for two 1,000-foot twin piers on Salmon Bay. Three other Port facilities also began taking shape in 1913. The Bell Street Pier was built that summer, and the first floor of the two-story wharf building was fully operational early in 1914. Even before that, 25 tons of Washington Chemical Works salsoda (sodium carbonate) was loaded from the Bell Street Pier onto a Victoria-bound vessel on October 28, 1913 — the first shipment to cross a Port of Seattle pier. The rest of the Bell Street facilities — the second floor of the wharf building and a separate large warehouse and cold storage building at the north end of the pier, which housed the Port offices on its top floor and featured a rooftop park and a viaduct connection to the Pike Place Market — were completed in 1915.

By late 1913, the first wharves and warehouses on the East Waterway pier also were in business, and the Port had built the wooden steamer *Leschi* for the Lake Washington

ABOVE: The steamship *Minnesota* is moored at the Great Northern Docks at Smith Cove in this postcard view.

BELOW LEFT: Fishermen's Terminal is dedicated, January 11, 1914.

RIGHT: The Port's ferry, *Leschi*, carried passengers and vehicles across Lake Washington before the advent of bridges.

SMITH COVE

In early 1853 Dr. Henry A. Smith arrived in the bustling village of Seattle. He'd crossed the Oregon Trail from Ohio, to Portland, Oregon Territory, in late 1852 and then had come north to check out opportunities on Puget Sound. Having heard of a proposed transcontinental railroad survey to the area, he paddled a dugout canoe from Olympia to scout the shoreline for the most probable site for a railroad to locate. He found the ideal sheltered cove along Elliott Bay nearly four miles north of Yesler's sawmill — a place with two villages the Duwamish people called called *silagwádsid* ("Talking: Mouth at Edge of Water") and *tʔə́kəp* ("Aerial Net for Snaring Ducks"). It would serve for constructing docks, and the flatlands behind could be developed as the tidewater terminus for the transcontinental railroad. So, Smith staked a 160-acre Donation Land Claim at a spot that soon became known as Smith's Cove and his mother made a claim on the adjacent plat just northward (today's Interbay area). As other newcomers trickled in, a good number agreed that the cove was a natural place for Seattle's future development and they bought residential lots on the two hills (today's Magnolia and Queen Anne) that flanked it to the west and east.

As he waited for those critical trains to arrive — they were the missing component that would allow Seattle to fully realize itself as a major seaport — Smith stayed busy. He cleared away trees, built a cabin on the western hillside, farmed, built and operated an infirmary, was appointed official physician for the Tulalip Indian Reservation, married and raised seven children, joined the Territorial Legislature — and consistently lobbied for a railroad to connect Seattle with the rest of the nation.

Following creation of the Port of Seattle in 1911, among the new agency's first priorities would be a 20-acre site (purchased for $150,000) that would come to be known as "Smith Cove." In 1913 the cove became home to Pier A, which was quite different than any then existing in the harbor. Rather than being built upon wooden pilings, the $1 million pier was framed with timber bulkheads, then center-filled with soil and rock dredged up from the adjacent slips. At approximately 2,530 feet long by 310 feet wide, Pier A was notable as the largest pier of its type yet built, and it conveniently provided berthage on both sides. That achievement was topped in 1920 by the Port's Pier B (later Pier 41). It was 2,580 feet long, built for $2,811,000, connected to eight tracks of the Great Northern Railway, and featured two huge warehouses that could hold two million cases of canned salmon, plus gantry and locomotive cranes, gas tractors, storage for up to 1.6 million gallons of oil, and waiting rooms for passengers cruising to the Orient.

This area would see much more history unfold, including the 1934 labor incident known as the Battle of Smith Cove and the U.S. Navy's takeover of the facilities (renamed as Piers 90 and 91) as a naval supply base during World War II. Today, Smith Cove's Terminal 91 provides docking facilities for Holland America Line, Princess Cruises, Royal Caribbean International, and Carnival cruise-ship lines, as well as for Seattle's factory trawler fleet for at-sea processing of seafood.

ABOVE TOP: An untitled painting of Smith Cove, ca. 1880s, by Emily Inez Denny.

ABOVE: Longshoremen load the vessel *Taiyu Maru* at Smith Cove, ca. 1916.

ABOVE: Silk from Japan, a lucrative cargo, is unloaded for swift transport to New York by rail.

LEFT: Smith Cove Cruise Terminal serves two ships at Pier 91, while Pier 90 accommodates factory ships of the North Pacific fishing fleet, in this contemporary view.

ABOVE TOP: Tractors ease the work of loading cargo at Smith Cove, ca. 1916.

ABOVE: Workers load lumber with a locomotive crane at Smith Cove, ca. 1916.

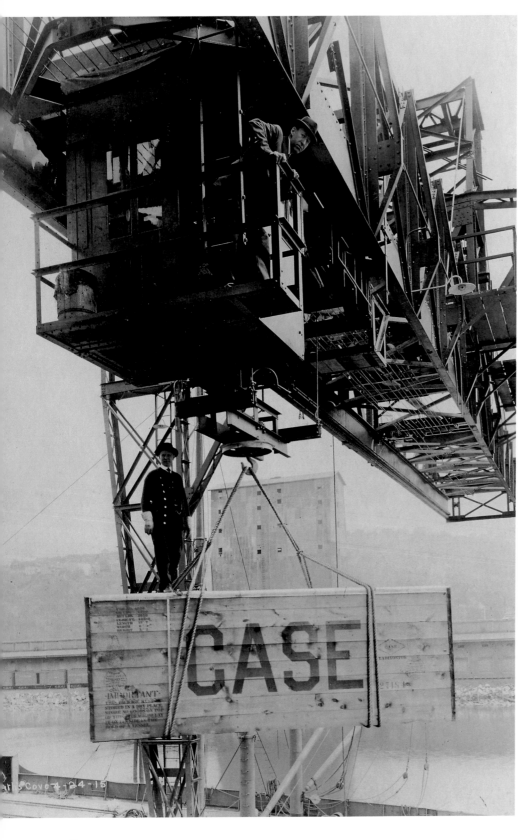

ferry route. The side-wheeler's maiden voyage, on December 27, 1913, marked two historic milestones: the *Leschi* was the first automobile ferry built in Western Washington, and the Port's ferry service was the first public, tax-supported water transportation in the Puget Sound region. (Although the Port pioneered public ferry service and briefly operated a few other routes, it transferred the ferries to King County before the end of the decade.) Also in December 1913, following discussions with farmers from Eastern Washington and Eastern Oregon, the commissioners initiated construction of a 500,000-bushel grain elevator on the East Waterway at Hanford Street to capture much of the grain trade that previously had followed the Columbia River to Portland.

From the start, Chittenden and Bridges made clear that the Port would set rates to promote trade, not to make a profit. Rather than charging "what the traffic will bear" like private enterprise, Chittenden explained, the Port would set wharf rates at "the lowest possible basis" on which port property could be maintained and the bonds paid off. Bridges concurred, saying, "we don't want dockage profit; we want low rates." Moreover, the commission began planning two public cold storage facilities, one for fruit and produce at the Bell Street Terminal, and one for fish on the East Waterway at Spokane Street. The former aided Eastern Washington farmers, making it easier for them to preserve and ship their produce. The latter was for local fishermen, providing lower rates than those offered by private cold storage facilities.

Led by Robert Bridges, the Populist former union organizer, the Port Commission also took a radically different approach to labor policy than did the private waterfront employers. The Port adopted the closed-shop rule — all longshore workers at Port facilities would be union members, and private employers who used Port facilities had to comply. Union workers loaded a Great Northern train for the first time in 1914, when members of International Longshoremen's Association (ILA) Local 38-12 moved 650,000 cases of canned salmon from ship to railcars across a Port dock. While Bridges remained on the commission, the Port's cooperation was reciprocated — during the bitter 1916 waterfront strike that shut down most shipping along the coast, the Port supported the union and Local 38-12 continued to work the Port's public docks.

These radical policies on rates and labor issues further angered the business establishment. Press criticism of the Port Commission continued unabated, and in 1915 the commission was among the targets of a new conservative-dominated legislature, which set out to undo as many progressive gains of the past years as it could. A bill was passed adding four new members to the commission (thus eliminating the authority of the current commissioners) and precluding the Port from issuing further bonds. Other new measures limited striking workers' ability to picket and rolled back the power of initiative and referendum. However, a coalition of progressive groups, including labor unions, the Municipal League, and the State Grange, united to force a referendum on seven of the new bills, preventing them from taking effect. Voters rejected all seven in 1916. By then, the Port's astounding commercial success had largely put an end to attacks on the commission.

Ironically, it was not the opening of the Panama Canal in August 1914, but another event that month — the outbreak of World War I in Europe — that actually led to explosive growth in Seattle's maritime trade. The canal itself brought relatively little trade until the end of the decade — first landslides, and then the war, kept it closed to most commercial traffic.

The war, on the other hand, by sharply reducing shipping on the Atlantic, produced a corresponding jump in Pacific trade. Vladivostok, Russia's largest port city on the Pacific Ocean, became a major destination, as Britain and France shipped supplies to Czarist Russia, their ally against Germany. The war also stimulated Japanese industrial development as the emerging Asian power provided large quantities of industrial goods for the Allied war effort.

Seattle captured the bulk of new shipping to both Russia and Japan, thanks in part to its geographic position — two days closer by ship than California ports — but mostly due to the Port's new facilities. With its large docks on the East Waterway and Smith Cove, Seattle could accommodate bigger ships and load them faster than San Francisco or other rival ports. The Smith Cove dock, which opened in April 1915, featured a large, train-track-mounted gantry crane that could do the work of 15 men and six horses, slashing loading time and cost so dramatically that shippers diverted bulk exports from ports up and down the coast to Smith Cove. The Port Commission's policy of cutting shipping rates, making Seattle the lowest-cost port on the coast, also contributed to its new dominance.

ABOVE TOP: Longshoremen load Samson Brand apples.

ABOVE: Schooners take on grain at Hanford Street Grain Terminal.

OPPOSITE: Gantry crane at Smith Cove, ca. 1916.

ROBERT BRIDGES

As one of the Port of Seattle's first commissioners (1911–1919), Robert Bridges brought to the table a hard-knuckled commitment to the progressive ideals of the Populist Era. Born in 1861 to a coal miner in Scotland, Bridges took to the mines at the tender age of 8 — and the brutal working conditions there encouraged him to lead a strike at age 9. His life-long commitment to seeking better conditions for the working class was thus deeply instilled.

Bridges and his bride emigrated to America in 1882, and five years later they had reached Black Diamond, Washington, where he found work in Pacific Coast Company coal mines. It was there that Bridges became a union organizer. In 1890 Bridges moved his family to Seattle where he opened a general store near the waterfront. With an angry political tide rising nationwide, Bridges fell in with the Populist Party, whose hearts he won after spurning a free travel ticket offered to politicians by the railroad. Instead, he *walked* from Seattle to the party convention across the mountains in the tiny ranching town of Ellensburg. Nominated for the position of state lands commissioner, Bridges was among the Populist candidates who swept the board in the 1896 election.

In 1900, the Bridges moved to Orillia (southwest of Renton) where they took up farming. He helped establish a drainage district in Orillia, and then focused on the underdeveloped lower Duwamish River area and for a time managed the Duwamish Waterway project. Then, when the concept of establishing the Port of Seattle arose, he declared as a candidate and on September 5, 1911, won the south district seat on its first commission. As Seattle historian Walt Crowley once noted, that election was "a high-water mark for the local Progressive Movement, which advocated public control of essential facilities and utilities, and a pivotal defeat for the railroads that had long dominated Seattle's harbor thanks to imprudent municipal concessions." Taking on the presidency of the Port Commission in 1915, Bridges joined the ongoing battles with renewed vigor.

Bridges was dead-set on forcing plenty of change. When the Supreme Court ruled that year that the Port Commission had to stop selling ice to fishermen, he declared that such sales — essential for small-time fishermen competing against the big operations that had their own ice-making facilities — would continue. And, acting against the best advice of port counsel,

Bridges demanded that all Port of Seattle longshoremen join a union. A class warrior who distrusted the motives and means of war policymakers in Washington, D.C., in 1916 Bridges also spoke up against a military buildup and even forbade Port employees to participate in Seattle's "Preparedness Day" parade. Then after the U.S. entered World War I and the costs of food suddenly skyrocketed, Bridges arranged for the Port's warehouses to store at minimal cost the goods of hardworking area farmers so they could avoid underselling to middlemen in a panicked rush. But political tides were shifting once again.

As war fever took hold, political progressives and labor were attacked as disloyal radicals. In the March 1917 election, Bridges backed a ballot measure calling for the Port's passenger-ferry system to provide free service, and he simultaneously pushed for the creation of a public market in Seattle where struggling locals could shop for affordable foodstuffs. Voters rejected both propositions. In time, Bridges began to be outvoted on various Port policies and measures, and he finally resigned from the commission in August 1919. But Bridges wasn't done fighting: In 1920 he was nominated for governor by the new Farmer-Labor Party. As one writer (at *Olyblog*) put it: "He was establishment enough to be taken seriously, but dangerous enough to instill fear into the hearts of all conservative newspaper editorialists and give them hyperbolic fits. He was a radical with credentials." Still, Bridges lost — though he did capture 30 percent of the vote — and went on to become a representative for the Seattle Longshoremen's Co-Operative and maintained his farm until he passed away on December 2, 1921.

Historian Padraic Burke noted that, "When the Port was under almost continuous criticism in the early years of its existence Bridges was frequently the Port's most eloquent defender. He consistently took the Port's case to the people of King County, where he and the Port were almost invariably sustained. Despite his criticism of the Seattle business community, he was a brilliant businessman for the Port. He crisscrossed the country, again and again, persuasively arguing the Port's case before groups of small and large businessmen, and he probably brought more business to the Port than any other individual during the first years of the Port's existence."

The statistics tell the story. In the second quarter of 1915, Washington surpassed all of California in foreign trade, $45 million to $41 million (Oregon had only $3.7 million). In 1916, Seattle far outpaced San Francisco in shipments to Asia. In 1918, Seattle set a tonnage record for foreign trade that it did not surpass until 1965, and was the second-busiest port in the entire country, behind only New York.

In addition to trade, the war gave a huge boost to Seattle's shipbuilding industry, not previously a large part of the region's economy. From 1916 to 1918, the federal government spent heavily on cargo and war ships, and eight Seattle shipyards employed 30,000 men working around the clock. The Skinner & Eddy yard alone churned out 75 freighters, 8,000 tons each, in an average of just 54 days apiece.

CONSOLIDATION AND COMPETITION

When the war ended, so did the Port's era of radical policies and equally radical growth. Chittenden had resigned in 1915, some months after Bridges supplanted him as president, and Remsberg lost his bid for reelection in 1918. Finding himself frequently outvoted by his new colleagues, Bridges stepped down in 1919. Subsequent commissioners were much more aligned with the conservative establishment than the original three had been, and the newspapers and business interests that had vehemently opposed early Port projects soon generally supported the commission and its initiatives.

Under this new leadership — W. S. Lincoln, George B. Lamping, and George Cotterill (author of the original port district legislation) comprised the commission for most of the 1920s — the Port abandoned many of the policies Bridges, Chittenden, and Remsberg had pursued earlier. It raised wharf rates to match those of private dock owners (though later in the decade it would face rate-cutting pressure from other public ports and even the railroads). Rather than developing and operating its own terminals, it encouraged local companies to lease Port land to build and run private terminals.

As soon as Lincoln replaced Bridges on the commission, he joined the Waterfront Employers Union (soon renamed the Waterfront Employers Association) and announced the Port would join private employers in hiring nonunion longshore workers. In response, Local 38-12 called a strike against the Port in May 1920. However, the ILA did not support the strike, and even the union local was divided. The strike failed disastrously. The Port became open shop like the rest of the waterfront, and there was little union activity until the bitter strikes of the Great Depression.

With the ILA moribund, the Waterfront Employers Association hired management consultant Frank Foisie to reform labor-management relations. Foisie created a joint representation plan whereby management and workers jointly operated hiring halls that selected dockworkers. Although this was essentially a company union (some workers derided the employer-dominated "fink halls"), working conditions in Seattle were better than at most other ports. Foisie's plan prohibited discrimination against ILA members (management elsewhere sought to rid the docks of union members), allowed workers to choose their representatives by secret ballot, and established a safety program.

One reason for the decline in union influence was the decrease in longshore jobs as Seattle's foreign trade fell from the record levels set during the war. For a few years, still-growing trade with Japan made up for the general international shipping decline that followed the end of World War I. In particular, nearly all the lucrative soybean oil trade from Japan passed through the Port's Smith Cove terminal — until Congress in 1921 imposed a high tariff that all but eliminated soy oil imports. In response, the Port initiated an aggressive marketing campaign in Japan and China, which helped reestablish Seattle as the leading port for raw silk imports. Great Northern's famous silk trains, which began serving Seattle in 1910, rushed the lucrative and fragile cargo from the Smith Cove

THE SEATTLE WATERFRONT
PIERSON & CO. Photo
© 1917

docks to the line's eastern terminus in Minnesota for onward shipment to New York City brokers, with 307 silk trains making the run between 1925 and 1932. Domestic trade and therefore total tonnage continued to grow through the 1920s, although at a slower pace than during the war years. The rise of highways, improvements in railroads, and use of oil pipelines all contributed to slow growth in maritime shipping.

In addition, the Port of Seattle faced increasing competition from other U.S. ports, engendered in part by Seattle's remarkable success in the previous decade. Impressed by what Seattle's public port had achieved, many other cities in Washington and around the country established publicly run ports of their own, often drawing on former Port of Seattle employees to build and run competing facilities. A former Port of Seattle chief engineer helped Los Angeles undertake a major harbor upgrade. Many competing Northwest ports built large grain elevators and cold storage facilities, recapturing market share in those areas. The competition was not just from the West Coast — the ports of Galveston and Houston took over almost all the cotton exports that Seattle had dominated.

Ironically, given the Port of Seattle's early emphasis on cutting dock rates, newer public ports like Tacoma's (which was created in 1918 and began shipping operations in 1921) slashed fees to win business from Seattle. The resulting price wars pitted public ports against each other, to the benefit of private shippers. Moreover, railroad companies cut their dock rates far below cost, seeking to bankrupt public ports and force them out of business. In 1929, the Port Authorities Association finally succeeded in setting uniform wharf rates, ending rate wars between public ports.

By then, the Great Depression was looming, and the steady, if modest, trade growth of the 1920s would soon be a distant memory.

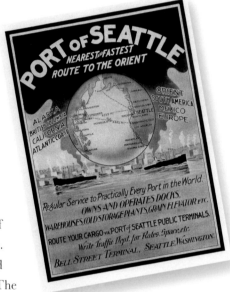

ABOVE TOP: Panorama of the Seattle waterfront, 1917.

ABOVE: Port of Seattle promotes its trade routes, Annual Report, 1928.

OPPOSITE ABOVE: Workers load raw silk bound for the East Coast.

BELOW: Silk trains met steamships at the Smith Cove docks to rush silk shipments onward to New York.

Chapter 3: **BOOM AND BUST**

T he Port of Seattle had worked hard throughout the decade of the
Roaring '20s to streamline its operations, refine its business model,
consistently reduce its tax levy, mount an aggressive advertising
campaign, and maximize the best usages of what had developed into some of
the finest port facilities on the Pacific Coast. Still, serious challenges lay ahead.
When the devastating financial news broke on "Black Tuesday," October
29, 1929 — the New York Stock Exchange had crashed — few could have
foreseen that this event portended the beginnings of a decade-long global
economic decline. The fallout would soon include profound unemployment,
slashed governmental spending, and even wage reductions for the luckily
employed. The only discernible upside to this bleak situation was that,
primarily because of diligent planning and the regional diversity of Seattle's
port, these negative effects were not quite as pronounced locally as they were
for other seaport cities. But there was plenty of woe all around.

OPPOSITE: Fishermen unload their salmon catch,
ca. 1920s.

THE GREAT DEPRESSION

The Pacific Northwest's economy had already been distressed before Black Tuesday arrived. Since prohibition had taken effect in Washington back in 1916 (with the adamant public cheerleading of soon-to-be Port Commissioner George Cotterill), many local breweries — including Seattle's iconic Rainier Brewery, which had long been the state's leading industrial employer — shut down, scaled back, or went into hibernation. Due to overfishing, the seafood industry was collapsing — the entire salmon catch of the 1920s was less than that taken in the record year of 1913. The timber industry also stagnated: Due to overproduction, local lumber mills — including those of Simpson, Weyerhaeuser, and Long-Bell — agreed to voluntarily cut hours or whole shifts to keep their crews working.

And things were about to get even worse. Economic hardships created a tense atmosphere all across America, fueling street gatherings of the disenchanted, some of whom became rabble-rousers crying for violent political revolution. Home foreclosures skyrocketed, and the ranks of the homeless increased with every day. Seattle's cheapest hotels and flophouses were maxed out, as the town became awash with desperate men and women who shuffled around town vainly seeking work. By late 1931, droves of homeless men began to squat on a large vacant patch of storied property owned by the Port of Seattle.

ABOVE: By 1937, nine billion board feet of lumber was produced and shipped from the Northwest annually.

RIGHT: Workers put labels on canned salmon, another of Washington's lucrative exports.

OPPOSITE CENTER: Hooverville, at the current location of Terminal 46, 1930s.

LEFT AND RIGHT: Hooverville just prior to final demolition, 1941.

BELOW: Hooverville's citizens elected a mayor and received mail.

HOOVERVILLE

A 206

A 207

As the Great Depression ground on, shantytowns began to arise in the hardest hit areas of America. In Seattle, they emerged along the banks of the Duwamish River, at "Louisville" on Harbor Island, and just behind Smith Cove (today's Interbay). But the largest and most infamous shack town grew on nine acres just south of Dearborn Street between Elliott Bay and Railroad Avenue (today the site of the Port's extremely productive Terminal 46 just west of Qwest Field sports stadium). Like many shanty towns built by homeless people during this time, it became known sarcastically as "Hooverville" in reference to U.S. President Herbert Hoover.

Originally the Hooverville acreage had been a mucky tide flat until reclaimed, in part, with sawdust and scrap fill from Henry Yesler's nearby lumber mill. Then in 1882 Robert Moran and his brothers founded a ship-repair business at the end of Yesler's Wharf. Both the shipyard and the wharf burned during the Great Fire of 1889, but within 10 days the Moran Brothers Shipyard was back up and running several blocks southward. This site later hosted the bustling Skinner & Eddy Shipyard's Plant 2 which produced many important ships during the boom times of World War I — and it was one of the initial flashpoint sites of the 1919 General Strike. But as the Depression deepened, Seattle's low-rent hotels, flophouses, and Skid Road missions filled beyond capacity, and in October 1931 the spillover of men began to build hovels in an area that held much history.

At one point, Washington Emergency Relief Administration investigator Donald Francis Roy reported that the site — which had become home to 1,000 inhabitants in 600 hundred shacks — featured "a conglomerate of grotesque dwellings, a Christmas-mix assortment of American junk that stuck together in congested disarray like sea-soaked jetsam spewed on the beach."

Twice over a period of months, the Seattle Police were sent in to evacuate everyone and torch

the village. Each time it soon rose again amidst the ashes and ruins. In June 1932 the distressed human inhabitants at Hooverville faced a committee of city officials who announced that the settlement would be tolerated — if a few rules were followed regarding proper sanitation, prohibiting alcohol, and not allowing women or children in. In addition, the inhabitants would be required to get out of their "gopher holes" and build true shacks. As unemployed logger Jesse Jackson (who was known as the "Mayor of Hooverville") recalled: "By this time the business houses had become more friendly to us and were very liberal with scrap lumber and tin, and the building of shanties got underway on a big scale. It seemed but a few short weeks until more than a hundred shacks were under course of construction."

A few years later, as WWII loomed and shipbuilding resumed, many Hooverville residents found jobs and the settlement began to fade away. The remaining men were evicted by the City in the spring of 1941 and on April 10, the abandoned Hooverville was finally bulldozed, and torched one last time. Two decades hence, the Port of Seattle made a farsighted commitment to redevelop the site into a vast loading apron that is now the site of the modern container-handling Terminal 46.

Ironically, eight decades after Hooverville's beginnings, economic hard times led to a revival of homeless tent camps on various sites, including in 2009 at a public shoreline park at the Port's Terminal 107. Demanding more public housing, the homeless and their advocates this time mockingly dubbed their settlement "Nickelsville" for Seattle Mayor Greg Nickels. Although sympathetic to their plight, the Port announced that habitation on that land was illegal and that the tent town would have to relocate. Port CEO Tay Yoshitani stated: "We continue to believe that the Port can best assist with the difficult problem of homelessness in our community by focusing on our mission to create jobs and economic growth for King County."

43

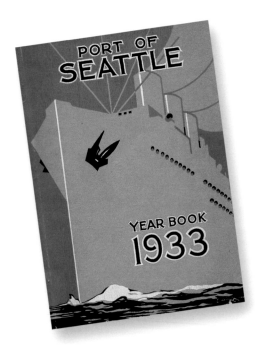

ABOVE: Port of Seattle Annual Report cover, 1933.

RIGHT: Washington State apples await shipment at Port warehouse, ca. 1920s. The Northwest had become the nation's largest producer of apples by 1937.

OPPOSITE TOP: Port Auditor Matt Gormley during his days in the Second Infantry.

BELOW: Railroad Avenue, renamed Alaskan Way, near Pier 70, during paving, 1934.

STREAMLINING AND SILK SALES

As the Depression deepened, Seattle politicians took to campaigning on the theme of streamlining the business of government, and the easiest target for such action was the salaries of public employees. Under such pressures, the Port tried to ensure that its 150 employees had some money coming in during the hard times. It announced pay cuts of up to 25 percent and instituted new measures, including cutting work hours, intended to decrease expenditures and increase productivity.

In 1932, the U.S. Congress passed the Smoot-Hawley Tariff Act in a misguided attempt to stabilize falling farm prices. The act ignited a backlash by various nations, whose in-kind retaliatory measures caused the international values of American goods to plummet. The Port of Seattle's core exports — apples, wheat, and salmon — dwindled to the extent that the elaborate cold storage facilities stood empty and unused. One of Seattle's most lucrative trades, Asian silk, dropped by 90 percent within five years. Still, other West Coast ports that were more heavily dependent on lumber exports, Tacoma and Portland among them, suffered even more.

But that fact gave no comfort to the Port, which just couldn't make up for drastically declining revenues. In each of these troubling years' annual reports, the commissioners attempted to strike notes of credible hope for the future, but by 1934 — five years into the Depression — they laid bare their souls, confessing that: "In 1932 we prayed for something to happen. In 1933 we just prayed." Still, the commissioners never wavered in their efforts. One initiative they launched to retain the domestic and foreign markets was an advertising outreach campaign in the huge Chicago and Asian markets. Locally, they won points in labor circles by maintaining full union pay scales for all longshoremen and stevedores — something the Waterfront Employers Association couldn't claim.

A NEW PORT COMMISSION

Yet for all the commissioners' efforts, an increasingly disgruntled public voted the entire Port Commission out of office between the years of 1932 and 1934, sweeping in a new crew who each ran on a platform of economizing Port operations. The complexities of administering the Port, however, ultimately led the new commissioners to govern with an approach similar to that of their predecessors — with the notable policy variation of opting to lease more Port properties to private businesses.

But the new administration's equilibrium was soon upset when a scandalous incident rocked the city. On Monday, May 8, 1934, the Port announced it had discovered a financial disparity in its accounting books. The following day, the *Post-Intelligencer* ran blaring headlines: "$70,000 Port Fund Shortage Bared; Auditor Gormley's Arrest Ordered." Matt Gormley — the Port's auditor — had reportedly been confronted at Port headquarters that morning and had then driven away, after saying he needed time to think and would return shortly. But when the citizenry opened their morning newspapers on May 10, they learned that Gormley — the brother-in-law of recently deposed but still serving Commissioner George Cotterill — had committed suicide in the Ravenna neighborhood. As the story played out over the following weeks, it seemed that Gormley had felt the weight of concealing various embezzlement schemes. Yet, it turned out that he personally had not stolen a cent. While the same could not be said of the Port's chief cashier (and his assistant), who may have made off with some of the missing money, Gormley instead had for 14 years been making occasional loans to Port employees to tide them over until their regular payday. These were well-intended loans that — with a little juggling of the books — were not necessarily paid back. But the clincher came when the investigation revealed that even Cotterill had given Gormley an IOU for a $190 loan — an IOU that became a political weapon for incoming Port Commission President J. A. Earley when it was discovered in a safe. Although there was no evidence that Cotterill had participated in a crime, Earley's grandstanding

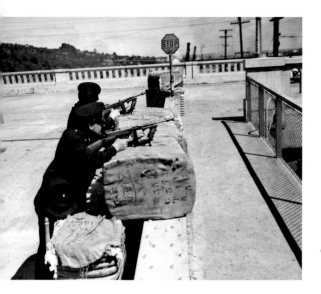

ABOVE: Police officers in position during the Battle of Smith Cove, 1934.

OPPOSITE: Strikers block a train during the Battle of Smith Cove, 1934.

succeeded in clouding the reputation of his otherwise highly regarded predecessor. As historian Padraic Burke wryly noted: "The only positive feature (and quite a small one at that) to come out of the entire Gormley affair was a resolution that the Port Commission adopted … to begin paying Port employees twice a month, instead of only once a month."

THE GREAT STRIKE OF 1934

Sharing the headlines in local newspapers that same May was a far more troubling story about ongoing and unprecedented maritime labor unrest, which came to involve the Port, transfix the whole city, and indeed, wrack the seaport towns of the entire West Coast. From May 9 to July 31, Seattle's harbor was paralyzed by a strike that poisoned labor-management relations for the following decade and a half. The struggle pitted the International Longshoremen's Association (ILA) against steamship owners, police, and hostile public officials, and it would prove to be one of the most significant and bitter clashes of the century.

The trouble was sparked when the Waterfront Employers Association (WEA) refused to negotiate with the ILA — triggering a strike down the entire coast. Led by Harry Bridges — a spirited Australian sailor and dockworker who had emigrated to America in 1920 and would remain active in union leadership for four decades — the workers struck to demand a coastwide contract with wage and hour improvements and an end to practices such as "the speed-up" (when workers were driven to work harder without commensurate pay) and "the shape-up" (when employers handpicked who would work each day). A key demand was the establishment of hiring halls run by unions, not bosses. In Seattle, members of ILA Local 38-12 and allied maritime unions concentrated on stopping trains serving the waterfront and blocking the use of strike-breaking "scabs" on the docks.

Initially, the longshoremen had broad union support, including that of the International Teamsters Union, which represented the workers who drove the horse wagons (and later trucks) that hauled away the goods unloaded from ships by the longshoremen. At that time, the teamsters' leader was Belltown's nationally famous tough-guy, Dave Beck. Though a standup union man through and through, Beck always believed that a strike should be labor's last resort — so Local 38-12 was no doubt ecstatic when he told teamsters not to cross ILA picket lines. However, that elation evaporated two days later when Beck — under intense pressure from politicians in Washington, D.C. — reversed his position. But the teamsters rebelled and ignored Beck's order to cross the longshoremen's lines. Nevertheless, his decision to yield sparked decades of hostility between the two union groups.

During the impasse, various local lumber mills were shuttered — with four closing for good — and shipping companies threatened to relocate to less turbulent Los Angeles. By mid-June, a tentative settlement was offered to ILA members for ratification. As they debated the proposal, newly installed Seattle Mayor Charles L. Smith decreed a "state of emergency" on June 14 and mobilized police to "open" the port, leading to a standoff with

UNION LONGSHORE WORKERS IN SEATTLE

The workers who unload the giant cargo ships at Port of Seattle marine terminals — truck drivers on the docks, cargo handling equipment operators, the cargo handlers in the holds, and the elite operators who maneuver the giant container cranes from small cabs slung under the crane booms — are all members of Seattle Local 19 of the International Longshore and Warehouse Union (ILWU), the heir and embodiment of a long, proud history of Seattle longshore unions.

Longshoremen were among the first workers in Washington to unionize, during the mid-1880s wave of organizing by the Knights of Labor and other activists. Longshore workers were motivated not just by low pay and the physical hardships and dangers of the job, but also by the insecurity of traditional hiring practices. Workers had to compete each day to be hired by stevedore bosses at early-morning "shape-ups," and favoritism and discrimination were rampant. During a March 1886 strike, Tacoma dockworkers organized the first longshore union on Puget Sound. Seattle longshoremen soon followed.

On June 12, 1886, three days into a strike demanding a pay raise to 40 cents an hour, striker Terry King gathered fellow workers in his small shack and they organized the Stevedores, Longshoremen, and Riggers Union (SLRU) of Seattle. Article 10 of the SLRU constitution set forth the fundamental principle of job control for which longshore workers would fight during the next half-century: in place of the hated shape-up, the union would dispatch men from its membership rolls, in strict alphabetical order, to work the ships. The strike ended late in June with most shipping companies on the Seattle waterfront accepting, at least temporarily, both union job control and the 40 cents an hour pay rate.

The early union gains were wiped out by the tough economic times of the 1890s. The SLRU essentially disappeared after losing an 1894 strike against a pay cut. In 1900, Seattle longshore workers affiliated with the International Longshoremen's Association (ILA), which had been formed in the 1890s by workers at ports on the Great Lakes. In 1909 West Coast longshore workers formed ILA District 38 as an autonomous branch of the ILA. The Seattle local became ILA Local 38-12, which would carry the union banner on Seattle docks through the great maritime strike of 1934.

Despite the years of organizing, however, longshore workers had made few permanent gains. Wages in 1915 were about the same as they had been in 1889 and bosses again controlled most hiring. In 1916, the ILA organized the first coastwide strike in West Coast history in an effort to win higher pay and more importantly a closed shop — an agreement allowing the hiring only of union members. Although the Port of Seattle acceded (and Local 38-12 kept Port docks working), private employers refused and after 74 days on the picket lines, ILA members returned to work, their demands unmet.

World War I accomplished what the 1916 strike did not. With trade at record levels and workers scarce, employers raised pay, agreed to an eight-hour workday, and (again temporarily) accepted the closed shop. But within a few years of the war's end, employers up and down the coast began rolling back the union advances. When the Port of Seattle followed suit, the unsuccessful 1920 strike in response fractured Local 38-12 and basically ended longshore union activity in Seattle for 14 years.

It was only with the union victory in the epic coastwide strike of 1934 that the long-desired goal of job control was permanently achieved. The arbitrated agreement that ended the strike established the union hiring hall that still exists today. Longshore workers start each day in the union local headquarters, where they peg in on one of several pegboards for different job classes, and are assigned out by a union dispatcher in the order they peg in, without regard to seniority or employer preferences.

In 1937, Harry Bridges, the Australian-born San Francisco longshore leader who played a lead role in the 1934 strike (he was no relation to early Port Commissioner Robert Bridges, although equally radical in his views), broke from the ILA and led most West Coast longshore locals into his newly formed International Longshoremen's and Warehousemen's Union. (When greater numbers of women began working on the docks, the ILWU modified its name to the current gender-neutral form.) Seattle's ILA Local 38-12 became ILWU Local 19.

Bridges headed the ILWU for the next four decades, building it into one of the most powerful unions in the nation's history and winning significant additional gains for dockworkers. Over fierce objections from some members, he negotiated the Mechanization and Modernization Agreement that paved the way for containerization and other innovations while ensuring that ILWU members would operate the new machinery.

The "M&M" agreement did not prevent job loss (ILWU membership dropped significantly over the years from its high of around 40,000) or end all labor conflicts — there were coastwide work stoppages in 1971 and 2002 — but it did usher in an era of significantly greater cooperation. Today, ILWU Local 19 functions much more as a partner with the Port and private companies in efforts to improve working conditions, boost production, and attract trade to Seattle.

CENTER: Longshoremen painstakingly load break-bulk cargo with cargo pallets and ship's gear — a vast difference from today's containers and 300-foot-high cranes.

CENTER INSET: An ILWU worker loads apples in a ship's hold at a Port container terminal, 1999.

TOP: ILWU members await job assignments at the hiring hall, 1981.

ABOVE: A worker moves cargo using an early forklift.

Strikers gather at the pier entrance during the Battle of Smith Cove, 1934.

pickets the following day. On June 16, all but the ILA's Los Angeles local rejected the terms of the draft settlement. Thus began the famous "Battle of Smith Cove."

THE BATTLE OF SMITH COVE

To prepare for expected conflict, the City of Seattle and King County had massed 300 city police, 200 "special deputies," and 60 state troopers, who were met at Piers 40-41 (now Terminal 91) by 600 unarmed pickets. Meanwhile, 18 ships waited off-shore to land their cargo, while a squad of scabs huddled aboard an old steamer at the end of the dock. On June 21, strikers halted a Great Northern train en route to the piers, and mounted police charged with clubs and tear gas. The workers stood their ground and carried the day. But subsequent confrontations turned uglier, with violence escalating at every major West Coast port.

Seattle saw ILA leader Shelvy Daffron killed and then King County Sheriff's Special Deputy Steve S. Watson disarmed by a crowd and shot with his own gun.

By this point, the economic effects of the strike were even starker: The ongoing labor unrest had brought waterfront commerce to a standstill. President Franklin Roosevelt and the National Longshoremen's Board (NLB) offered to arbitrate an end to the strike. On July 21, union members voted to accept their proposal, and strikers all along the coast went back to work on July 31. The arbitration decision, issued in October, granted wage increases to 95 cents an hour (the workers had wanted $1) for straight time and $1.50 for overtime, a shorter week of 30 hours, and a six-hour day. In addition, it established that the "hiring of all longshoremen shall be through halls maintained and operated jointly," but "the dispatcher shall be selected by the International Longshoremen's Association." This was a major victory. The ILA had won virtually all its demands, and the arbitration result firmly established the rights of waterfront workers nationwide.

LABOR STRIFE CONTINUES

But just a few years later — on January 5, 1938 — 1,500 Seattle longshoremen struck again in a dispute over the interpretation of a year-old contract with the WEA. All movement of cargo across the Seattle waterfront ceased, and the Port of Seattle necessarily shut down. For a week, ships were diverted to Tacoma and other ports for unloading, until U.S.

Maritime Commission Chairman Joseph P. Kennedy (father of future U.S. President John F. Kennedy) stepped in and this latest dispute was submitted to the NLB for arbitration.

Such crises earned Seattle the reputation in business circles as the least cooperative port town on the coast, and its port would decline in the decades ahead. Indeed, the city as a whole stagnated during the Great Depression. Seattle's population had nearly tripled from 80,871 to 237,174 between 1900 and 1910; between 1910 and 1920, it grew to 315,685 (about 33 percent); but in the 1930s, it increased by fewer than 3,000 people. For all the desperate transience of the American populace during those terrible days, the mobile and migratory had little reason to come to Seattle.

THE WAR YEARS

The first rumblings of war in Europe in 1939 brought back frightful memories of World War I. Direct effects included the withdrawal of various foreign trade partners and shipping companies, as well as trade embargoes that caused a contraction of business activity at the Port. In particular, the shipment of scrap iron to Japan from Seattle — which had been one bright spot in the depressed economy of the 1930s — was instantly halted. Also stymied was another of the Port's key exports — Eastern Washington's famous apple crop, whose main overseas market had been Europe.

German submarine attacks on ships of all flags crossing the Atlantic Ocean had a twofold impact on business. The first was to severely reduce the shipping tonnage of American ports in general. The second was to spark a need for increased American shipping across the Pacific with Siberian Russia — a change that actually resulted in a sizable uptick in business based in Seattle. In addition, the Maritime Commission awarded Harbor Island–based Seattle-Tacoma Shipbuilding Corporation a $10.6 million contract to build five C-1 freighters. When the U.S. government launched a crash program to rearm the U.S. Navy and the merchant marine services with new ships, the same firm scored a huge contract to build 20 destroyers. This new maritime activity represented the beginning of a historic boom.

Additional governmental actions altered the Port's fortunes. In March 1941, the U.S. Navy initiated a takeover of the enormous Piers 40 and 41 at Smith Cove, which were recognized as the largest of their type in the world, and which remained the most massive in America for many years. Even though America had not yet joined the distant war, the regional economy was already humming. The unemployment rate had fallen to a point that Seattle's Hooverville had become an anachronism. Accordingly, in April 1941, Port commissioners — now seeing a need for more space to conduct rapidly increasing maritime business — ordered that the shanty town be bulldozed to make way for a major new terminal.

Earlier that year, the Washington State Legislature, as part of efforts to ensure adequate wartime preparedness, enacted a law granting new powers to port districts — including one to issue without public approval revenue bonds to finance the construction

TOP: Sailors march across the Bell Street Pier viaduct, ca. 1930s. Bell Street Pier, today's Pier 66, was the original Port headquarters.

ABOVE: Hanford Street Grain Terminal, with a capacity of 1.5 million bushels, served as Seattle's main export site for Eastern Washington and Midwest grain from 1915 to 1970.

ABOVE: A family is reunited when a World War II ship returns to Seattle. During World War II and the Korean War, thousands of sailors and soldiers shipped out and came home through Seattle's Army Port of Embarkation, then located at Piers 36, 37, 38, and 39.

ABOVE RIGHT: Troops line up to board ship at the Port of Embarkation.

OPPOSITE TOP: Port of Seattle Commission President Horace Chapman, Port of Tacoma Commission President Fred Marvin, U.S. Representative (later Senator) Warren Magnuson, and Governor Arthur Langlie break ground on January 2, 1943, for the airport at Bow Lake, soon to be called Seattle-Tacoma International Airport.

BOTTOM: Port officials celebrate the first landing on the new runway at Sea-Tac, October 31, 1944.

of piers, wharves, terminals, warehouses, and other improvements for national defense. Although it raised concerns that the Port would now face less public scrutiny, the new authority enabled the Port to purchase Harbor Island's East Waterway Dock and to begin construction of the new $2.8 million Pier 42 (today included as part of Terminal 46). The project was notable for the sheer quantity of landfill required. The bay was so deep at this section that 60 feet of dredging spoils from adjacent slips was dumped in. Then hundreds of 40- to 70-foot pilings were driven in. Finally, the face of the bulkhead comprised 82- to 120-foot creosote-treated timbers. Upon that substructure, the Port built two 1,000-foot-long sheds and many modern facilities that were unprecedented on Seattle's waterfront. In addition, the Port built a $335,000 grain elevator at the Hanford Street facility.

In July 1941, Franklin Delano Roosevelt signed a presidential order halting trade with one of Seattle's biggest partners, Japan, whose warring aggression in Asia had become unacceptable. Then, after America entered the war following the December 7, 1941, Japanese attack on Pearl Harbor, Seattle's waterfront itself was radically transformed. The U.S. military effectively took control of the entire harbor to aid the war effort, imposing a new numbering system to help make better sense of the illogically named array of piers, wharves, and terminals that had sprouted over the previous nine decades. Most significantly, the piers at Smith Cove became Piers 90 and 91. On the central waterfront, the Port's Bell Street Pier officially became Pier 66. The Army rebuilt the Pacific Steamship Company Terminal as Pier 36 and built Piers 37, 38, and 39. Those four piers collectively became an official Port of Embarkation for the duration of the four-year war (today, that area comprises part of Terminal 46, with Pier 36 remaining the U.S. Coast Guard base).

Although the government's announcement in February 1942 placing all coastal ships in war service obliterated normal commercial activities in Seattle's harbor and elsewhere, the outbreak of war instantly fired up other sectors of the local wartime economy. The military needed aircraft, and Seattle's Boeing Airplane Company (now The Boeing Company) quickly ramped up to produce warplanes, including the mighty B-17 and B-29 bombers. Also, Seattle's shipyards and docks became a magnet for an influx of civilians to the Northwest, most arriving with the fervent hope of putting the Depression years behind them with new, well-paying jobs.

A NEW DUTY: BUILDING AN AIRPORT

Besides taking over most of the waterfront, the military was soon monopolizing the region's airports. Even before Pearl Harbor, increasing bomber production clogged Boeing Field, which, although named for the airplane manufacturer, was then King County's main commercial airport. The growing demands on Boeing Field, and the aviation hazards posed by the high ridge to its east, had already prompted calls for a new airport. The same 1941 legislative session that expanded public ports' ability to issue bonds also specifically authorized ports to build and operate airports. After the U.S. entered the war and the military took control of Boeing Field, McChord Field in Pierce County, and Paine Field in Snohomish County, the federal Civil Aeronautics Administration (CAA) offered $1 million to any local government that would undertake the task of building a new regional airport. The Port of Seattle promptly stepped forward.

Port Commission President Horace Chapman asserted that building the airport "is our duty, and if we can do it, we will." The commission voted in March 1942 to build the new field on 907 acres of forest and scrubland at Bow Lake, midway between Seattle and Tacoma. The choice of location and the name — Seattle-Tacoma Airport (quickly nicknamed Sea-Tac) — followed agreement by the City of Tacoma, the Port of Tacoma, and Pierce County to contribute $100,000 if the airport was located to serve, and was named for, Tacoma as well as Seattle. The CAA took charge of constructing the airport and its four runways (a primary north-south runway, a shorter east-west strip, and two crosswind runways forming an X), which were completed in 1944.

Despite a ceremonial first landing by a United Air Lines DC-3 on October 31, 1944, and inauguration of transcontinental passenger service by Northwest Airlines the following spring, Sea-Tac saw little commercial use until 1946. Instead, the Army Air Force used the new airport for transshipment of thousands of Boeing B-29 bombers.

Chapter 4: **INTO THE JET AGE**

The extreme wartime hustle and bustle along Seattle's waterfront gradually eased back to a calmer pace after the war ended with Japan's surrender on August 15, 1945. Although peace was welcomed by a war-weary nation, the transition back to a peacetime economy proved surprisingly tough, and the Port of Seattle faced daunting challenges.

Just five years prior, Seattle's Boeing Airplane Company had entered its booming years as part of President Franklin D. Roosevelt's "arsenal of democracy" by providing thousands of aircraft to the U.S. military — a task that allowed the firm to grow into the largest employer in the region. When the contracts for bombers were canceled at war's end, Boeing was forced to cut 70,000 employees. Another blow came when the expected postwar surge in imports and exports through the Port of Seattle failed to materialize. The stagnant business was partly due to the growth of the trucking industry and expanded rail services, but some critics also blamed passive Port leadership.

OPPOSITE: Seattle-Tacoma Airport is an impressive sight with its grand drives and art deco architecture, 1950s.

THE SHIPPING SLUMP

At war's end — and with the subsequent dismantling of various international trade embargoes and tariffs — it was hoped that a sense of normalcy would develop in commerce. But even as defense-related activity subsided, commerce through the Port failed to revive from the steady decline that had begun during the Depression. Though the national economy had expanded greatly since then, the Port's share of world trade, relative to the nation's other ports, was now less than 50 percent of what it had been just 15 years prior. In particular, Seattle saw its shipping business fall behind its longtime competitor Tacoma and other ports it had previously far outranked. Critical observers of the Port attributed the decline to uninspired leadership and questioned the usefulness of some projects. Another criticism regarded the Port's lack of an aggressive advertising and promotion program. As historian Padraic Burke noted: "While other U.S. ports [had] embarked on far-sighted programs to lure an increasing share of world trade to their harbors, most of the Port of Seattle's programs seemed to be ill-conceived and haphazardly executed."

The Port's commissioners — being fiscally conservative men, in general — were initially reluctant to launch expensive endeavors. However, some major changes to the central waterfront were driven by historical forces. When the U.S. military's use of various piers subsided at war's end, some reverted to commercial use, but such change was not always positive for the community or the Port. For example, in the immediate postwar years, Seattle's shipping industry naturally migrated to the Duwamish and Harbor Island facilities south of downtown, and soon the central waterfront fell into decline and disrepair. In fairness to Port leadership, the emergence of new transportation systems — not to mention the sudden availability of job-seeking military veterans — was bound to affect the general economy, including the maritime shipping industry.

POSTWAR LABOR STRIFE

The fact that Harry Bridges and his International Longshoremen's and Warehousemen's Union (ILWU) had closed ranks with ship owners at the war's outset — an admirable alliance that focused on increasing productivity to aid the war effort — meant less to both sides as World War II wound down and the Cold War with the Soviet Union commenced. Bitter feelings — stemming all the way back to the 1934 Battle of Smith Cove — reemerged with a series of disputes that led to a coastwide 48-day strike beginning in October 1946.

In June 1947, the U.S. Congress passed the Taft-Hartley Act — a measure that tilted the power equation back from the unions to management. Hard-won gains that the unions had enjoyed since the 1930s were upset, and when contract renewal time came the following year, the WEA was emboldened enough to demand control of the hiring hall. On September 1, 1948, a 95-day strike began, a bitter action that halted all shipping on the Pacific Coast. One tactic the WEA used to break union members' resolve was to announce it would not negotiate with union leaders who refused to sign an affidavit declaring they were not communists. A long siege began with each side hoping to outlast the other. Then one company reconsidered: Seattle's Griffiths & Sprague Stevedoring Co. cut a special deal with the ILWU — granting a significant wage increase and tacitly acknowledging the union's control over the hiring hall. With the stalemate now partially breached, the Port of Seattle followed suit about two weeks later and likewise acceded to the union's demands.

Leaders of the WEA, however, remained adamant that they could not deal with Bridges, whom they condemned as a "communist." It seemed that an outside force would be required to break the jam — and that came in the wake of the upset election of President Harry Truman on November 6. Within days, the WEA, under pressure from some member companies that faced bankruptcy, sent in new negotiators, and on November 25, an agreement was hammered out that left the ILWU in its most powerful position ever. The severely weakened WEA desperately merged with the American Shipowners Association the following year in a move that produced the Pacific Maritime Association. The major downside for the victorious union was that the 1948 strike had fortified the reputation Seattle's waterfront had gained as a radicalized trouble spot. Business interests naturally began to consider expanding their use of the trucking industry instead. In response, union and management tried to repair some of this damage by publicly playing nice, but behind the scenes, the struggles continued.

ACQUISITION AND EXPANSION

In the postwar era, the Port of Seattle responded to newly emerging opportunities with the twin goals of stabilizing local employment levels and making its own activities and facilities increasingly efficient and modern. In 1946, the Port embarked on a $22 million,

ABOVE: Strikers hold signs reading "Our Union Today, Your Union Tomorrow" and "We are Ready to Work" at a terminal entrance, Seattle, 1947.

OPPOSITE TOP: Smith Cove docks, renumbered as Piers 90 and 91 by the U.S. military, in 1944.

BELOW: Special edition 1944 Port of Seattle *Victory Book*.

FISHERMEN'S TERMINAL

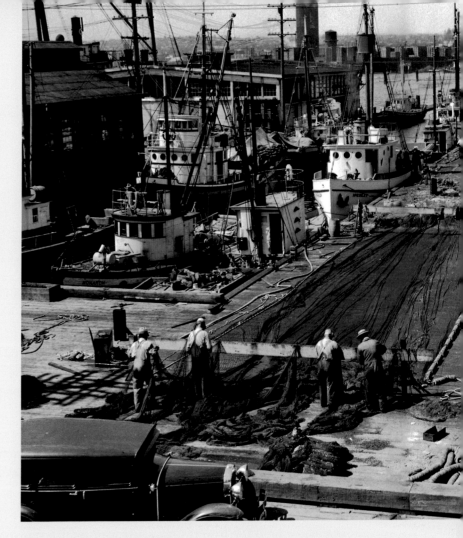

Fishermen's Terminal on Salmon Bay — the last major in-city wharf in America long dedicated to fishing boats — is one of the Port of Seattle's crown jewels. Salmon Bay itself — linked to freshwater Lake Union to the east and via a narrow creek (called "the outlet" by early settlers) to the saltwater of Puget Sound to the west — was a rich native fishing ground for centuries. Non-Indian settlers — like Edmund Carr, whose land claim south of the bay would ultimately be the site of Fishermen's Terminal — also depended on the waters of Salmon Bay and beyond. The newcomers included many Norwegian and other Scandinavian immigrants whose subsequent livelihood would help define their new home's image and economy: fishing. Because that community of fishermen largely settled in the bordering town, Ballard, they moored their vessels on the bay at privately owned marinas.

Soon after the Port was born in 1911, its first commissioners began to envision building a deep-sea cargo facility at Salmon Bay. But in 1913 an association of immigrant fishermen complained about getting gouged on mooring fees by private dock-owners. The Port was told that unless it provided them with a drydock facility, the entire industry would move to a different town. The Union Pacific Railroad stepped up and gifted the fishing fleet a strip of land (with the Port named as caretaker), area voters approved a public bond issue to finance construction, and on January 11, 1914, the Salmon Bay Terminal opened. Amid great fanfare Commissioner Hiram Chittenden gave a grand speech describing the new facility's mission: "To organize and solidify the scattered fishing industry of the Northwest, to provide a home for the extensive fishing fleet, to give such aid as the Port rightfully should give in protecting the fisherman in marketing his hard-earned products — this surely is an ambition worthy of the most earnest efforts of the Port Commission."

The terminal would eventually boast mooring floats, piers, docks, net lockers, and warehouses — along with boat-building and repair plants. In May of 1952, the Port completed a major, million-dollar expansion and modernization of what had long been redubbed Fishermen's Terminal — establishing it as the finest commercial fishing moorage facility in the country. Soon the bulk of the entire Alaska fishing fleet — which at that point consisted of 1,000 vessels — settled in, and Seattle began benefiting from the industry's multi-million-dollar annual contribution to the economy. Two new 625-foot piers had been built, as were two new net sheds; 25 acres for future expansion were added to the west; and a massive dredging operation improved the whole facility. The early 1950s also saw the rise of Byron and Helen Horton's venerable restaurant called The Wharf, which naturally featured a seafood-based menu along with a large live music dance lounge that drew crowds for decades. Waves of redevelopment upgrades began in the 1970s and today the terminal facility boasts 227,000 square feet of warehouse and light industry, office, and commercial retail space, including popular attractions like Chinooks Restaurant, the Highliner Pub, and the Wild Salmon Seafood Market.

In 1988 — the same year that the Port invested $13 million in improvements to Fishermen's Terminal — it became the home of the Seattle Fishermen's Memorial, a towering bronze and stone sculptural monument erected in honor of the more than 675 local men and women who have lost their lives pursuing commercial fishing since the beginning of the twentieth century. Yet that proud sense of maritime heritage also has sparked certain skirmishes. As the 1990s wound down — and the fishing fleet itself dwindled (the 371-slip facility had more than 100 vacant slips) — Port leadership began to believe that some economic diversification was necessary to sustain the terminal's economic viability.

In 2001 one controversy erupted after a consultant's report advised that the Port could raise additional revenues (required for an estimated $60 million terminal upgrade, admittedly needed due to deferred maintenance) by allowing some yachts and other pleasure-craft to moor there. Port leaders stressed the fishing industry's essential role in the local economy and the Port's commitment "to support the industry and meet the changing needs of the fleet." Nonetheless, a community watchdog group — the Friends of Fishermen's Terminal — alarmed about potential gentrification, unsuccessfully challenged the new moorage policy plans. Thus, today the piers are home to a mix of private boats and commercial ships (which annually generate somewhere upward of 5,000 jobs and more than $400 million in wages and business revenues) — and Fishermen's Terminal remains a key fixture of both the past and present, one that has exuded a certain romantic aura for generations of Seattleites. With a $7 million electrical upgrade completed and aged wooden docks replaced with floating concrete, the Port engaged stakeholders in 2009 and 2010 to develop a 20-year plan for the terminal to ensure that the evolving needs of the fishing fleet are met.

decadelong expansion program that produced many major projects. Among the most notable were the $2 million acquisition (from the Pacific Coast Company) and modernization of Piers 43 and 45 to 49 just south of the central waterfront (all but Piers 48 and 49 later would be incorporated into the container mega-terminal at Terminal 46), the $1 million enlargement and upgrading of the Salmon Bay Fishermen's Terminal (which contributed $50 million in annual income to the local economy), and the $5 million modernization of the East Waterway dock on Harbor Island.

But again, the Port's priorities were criticized. It was noted that such projects were mounted at a time when the Port's properties lacked adequate grain storage facilities, and the export market for that key commodity from Eastern Washington was thus rapidly shifting to Tacoma and Portland. The Port invested much time and capital into establishing a Foreign Trade Zone on Harbor Island that failed to generate the additional business activity touted by the agency's leadership. Such a zone would provide an area where businesses could repackage or relabel imported goods without incurring prohibitive duty fees, which instead would be levied at the final destination. Business interests supported the concept — one embraced by only a handful of other American ports — and after five years of intense lobbying by the Seattle Chamber of Commerce, the Port finally authorized the zone in May 1949. Then, on September 1, the Foreign Trade Zones Board granted the necessary charter. Existing facilities at the East Waterway were improved and Seattle's Foreign Trade Zone opened for business. What had not been adequately foreseen, however, was the amount of land required to operate a practical zone, and the additional customs agents and officers needed — an expense that would be shouldered by the Port. It was a no-win situation that soon saw the same business interests that had pushed for the zone demanding that the Port shutter it.

ABOVE: The Port actively promoted its new Foreign Trade Zone No. 5 to potential customers after its 1949 opening. A model showcases imported goods in 1962. The trade zone served importers who needed space to store and prepare goods for market without incurring taxes and customs fees.

OPPOSITE, CLOCKWISE FROM TOP LEFT: Postcard view of fishing boats moored at the public fishermen's dock, Salmon Bay, ca. 1914.

CENTER: Fishermen lay out nets for repair at Fishermen's Terminal, 1936.

LOWER TOP: Fishermen's Terminal, 1913.

LOWER BOTTOM: Fishermen's Terminal, 2004.

TOP: The first air traffic control tower goes up at Bow Lake (Sea-Tac Airport), 1944.

ABOVE: Architect's plans for the 1949 Seattle-Tacoma Airport terminal.

BUILDING FOR THE JET AGE

In contrast to the lagging seaport, Sea-Tac Airport began growing as soon as civilian use resumed, and did not stop. Almost continuous construction was needed to keep pace with demand, but the investments paid off, and the airport was one of the few financial bright spots for the Port during the 1950s. When commercial passengers returned in 1946, terminal facilities consisted of old barracks and a Quonset hut restaurant called "The Pantry," heated by a potbellied stove. Recognizing that such primitive accommodations would hardly meet the anticipated postwar surge in air travel, the commission placed a $3 million bond issue on the November 1946 ballot to fund a new terminal and administration building. The bonds won a sizable majority, but insufficient voters turned out to validate the election, forcing the Port to turn to its reserves for funding.

A dedication ceremony on July 9, 1949, celebrated both the completion of the new administration building and the official naming of what would henceforth be Seattle-Tacoma *International* Airport. The gleaming white building with its soaring control tower and airy, glass-walled passenger concourses was hailed as America's most advanced airport terminal. Regularly scheduled airline service at Sea-Tac had begun two years earlier in 1947, but it was only after the new terminal opened that Northwest, United, and Western airlines shifted the bulk of scheduled passenger service from Boeing Field to Sea-Tac. Almost immediately, rapidly rising traffic volumes strained runway capacity. In 1950, the Port commenced the first of several extensions of the primary north-south runway, lengthening it to 7,500 feet.

As the airport work proceeded, Boeing, which had already successfully produced jet-powered bombers, was beginning to explore development of a passenger jet. British and Russian manufacturers had produced jet airliners earlier, but it was the Boeing 707, first flown as the Dash-80 on July 15, 1954, that became the prototype for large jet airliners and soon revolutionized travel. Much larger and faster than propeller-driven planes, the jets also required longer runways, and the Port added first 80, and then another 170, acres to Sea-Tac and extended the main runway another 1,000 feet. With new lights and aircraft surveillance radar installed, Sea-Tac inaugurated regular jet airliner service on October 3, 1959, when a Pan Am 707 took off for Honolulu.

THE PORT IN THE 1950S

Meanwhile, the Port's lackluster advertising and promotion of Seattle's considerable harbor facilities attracted criticism once again. It was not until the 1950s that the Port even established a public relations department. When the Port did promote itself, it seemed to believe that it was adequate to simply point out — as it had during the prewar years — that Seattle was the closest American port to Asia. But a number of factors had by now made that boast less relevant. Chief among them was the decision by the U.S. Maritime Commission and the Interstate Commerce Commission to help offset Seattle's geographical advantages by instituting a new sliding scale of shipping rates that favored formerly disadvantaged ports.

Another blow came with the release of the Municipal League's 1950 report, which clearly documented a five-year decline in Port revenues since the war's end.

By 1952 — a year that saw a full 100 days of productivity lost to strikes in Seattle — business activity at most other ports had rebounded to levels not seen since prior to the Great Depression. Not so for Seattle, where the Port reported very slim profits.

That same year brought the election of two new port commissioners, Clarence H. Carlander and Gordon Rowe, but the infusion of new blood heralded not unity, but more division in the leadership. Not only did the new commissioners begin feuding with each other, they also began butting heads with Port General Manager Warren Lamport. In August 1953, the Port Commission abruptly announced that it was abolishing Lamport's position and that the commission would take over day-to-day administrative duties. Publicly aired charges of waste and incompetence flew back and forth between the warring parties; reputations suffered and the Port's business languished.

Weeks later, however, the Port hired the Seattle-based district manager of the American Hawaiian Steamship Company, Howard M. Burke, as its general manager. Despite the acrimonious atmosphere, he quickly focused on the challenges the Port faced. Burke saw that the Port needed a unified program of modernization and development to take it into the modern age. Among the projects he initiated during the 1950s were

continued on page 66

ABOVE LEFT: Ethiopian Emperor Haile Selassie addresses a crowd at Sea-Tac, 1954. From its beginning, Sea-Tac became a place to welcome dignitaries and celebrate events.

RIGHT: Postcard of the newly opened airport terminal.

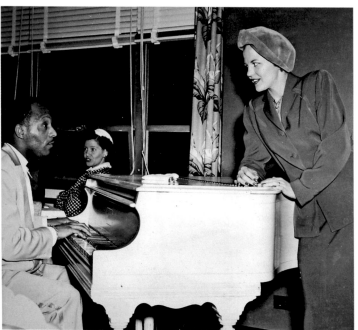

ABOVE: Sea-Tac was all about elegance, offering the traveler fine dining, a barbershop, a gift shop, and even a lounge with jazz pianist and singer, 1950.

LEFT: The original main terminal offered a spacious waiting area, a view of the airfield, and comfortable couches and armchairs.

SEA-TAC ADMINISTRATION BUILDING 1949

Sea-Tac came into its own as a full-service international airport on July 9, 1949, with the dedication of its modern new Administration Building. The four-story, 234,000-square-foot office and terminal complex replaced the makeshift array of World War II-era buildings that had served Sea-Tac's first airline passengers. Planning for the Administration Building began as soon as Sea-Tac returned to civilian use in 1946, and construction was well underway by the time Northwest Airlines and Western Airlines inaugurated Sea-Tac's first regularly scheduled flights in the fall of 1947.

Colonel Earle S. Bigler, who managed Sea-Tac for the Port in 1947, supervised the project. Herman A. Moldenhour and Port of Seattle Chief Engineer George T. Treadwell designed the structure, and Lease and Leighland General Contractors built it. The Administration Building, which also housed the passenger terminals, contained offices for Port staff, the airlines, the Civil Aeronautics Administration, and customs and immigration officials. It included a weather bureau, the airport control tower, a post office, and waiting areas, concourses, an observation deck, gift and coffee shops, and other amenities for passengers. Eight airplanes at a time could load and unload at the building.

Ground traffic reached the Administration Building from Highway 99 (Pacific Highway) east of the airport, via an access road that ended in a circular drive in front of the building. The building was located just east of Sea-Tac's main north-south runway, and near the center of the X formed by the two crosswind runways. The two wings of the building, shaped like an inverted V, paralleled those two runways where they extended northeast and southeast across the main runway. Sea-Tac's initial runway configuration, with the crosswind runways angling across the main runway and a perpendicular east-west runway at the south end, was typical of military airfields of the time. Runways facing various directions were necessary because aircraft then were less capable of landing in crosswinds than those of later years (by the 1960s, the crosswind runways were no longer used).

The Administration Building cost about $4 million, bringing the total cost of Sea-Tac construction to $11 million by the time the airport was dedicated. The July 9, 1949, ceremony celebrated both the completion of the new building and the official dedication of Sea-Tac as Seattle-Tacoma International Airport. A crowd of more than 30,000 people turned out for the festivities. Port officials, the mayors of Seattle and Tacoma, and other

dignitaries spoke from a flag-draped balcony. In the main address, Washington Governor Arthur Langlie declared:

> Man, on Puget Sound can now tell the eagles, the hawks, and skylarks to move over and say "We, too, have at last won our place beside you in the firmament of heaven."

Any birds around probably did move over as military aircraft roared repeatedly above the Administration Building to salute the dedication. Newly developed jet fighters dazzled the crowd with their speed, while bombers, troop carriers, and patrol planes also passed overhead. On the ground, spectators waited in long lines for closer views of the newest military and commercial aircraft, which were displayed on the airport loading ramps.

Until the Administration Building was completed, most scheduled passenger flights had operated from Boeing Field. With the opening, the four airlines then serving Seattle and Tacoma — Northwest, United, Pan

American, and Western — shifted the bulk of their flights to Sea-Tac. Within five months of the dedication, the airport was serving 1,500 passengers per day on 60 scheduled flights.

Those figures were just the beginning. As the numbers of both flights and passengers increased dramatically over the years, the Port steadily expanded Sea-Tac's facilities. From the late 1950s through the mid-1960s, four concourses were added to the main building, increasing the number of airplane gate positions to 21. As the concourses extended north and south, and with newer airplanes better able to handle crosswinds, the crosswind and perpendicular runways were eliminated, while the north-south runway was repeatedly lengthened (two parallel runways were later added).

Eventually, in the words of Seattle historian Paul Dorpat, the ever-growing facilities "swallowed" the 1949 Administration Building. In 1973, the Port opened a new, greatly expanded terminal building, which was constructed over and around the original structure. By the end of 2005, a capital improvement program including a new concourse and central terminal yet again changed the look and space of the facility.

CLOCKWISE FROM TOP LEFT: The first airport terminal, 1947.

CENTER: Visitors by the thousands came to celebrate the dedication of the new terminal on July 9, 1949.

TOP RIGHT: Sea-Tac initially had four cross-wind runways designed for airplane landings and takeoffs in almost any wind direction. The jet age soon ushered in parallel runways.

CENTER RIGHT: A crowd of visitors tours a Northwest Airlines aircraft during the dedication of the terminal, July 9, 1949.

BOTTOM RIGHT: Northwest Airlines flight attendants pose during the dedication festivities.

CENTER INSET: Postcard view of the Sea-Tac Administration Building, 1949.

TOP: Surveyor at Shilshole, preparing for construction of the marina, 1957.

ABOVE: An early aerial photo of Shilshole Bay Marina, 1963. The marina was dedicated during the Century 21 Exposition, the 1962 Seattle's World Fair.

the construction of a $2.6 million grain elevator addition to the Hanford Street facility; the building of a 1,500-boat public saltwater facility along the western edge of the Ballard neighborhood — Shilshole Bay Marina (which boasted a public fishing pier, and in later decades a popular public promenade more than a mile long); the $850,000 purchase of the Ames Terminal on the west side of the West Waterway (now part of Terminal 5); the $600,000 purchase of Pier 28 (from the Chicago, Milwaukee, St. Paul & Pacific Railroad); and the subsequent $8 million development of a large, modern terminal between Piers 28 and 30.

While most of Burke's idea's were welcomed by area business interests — who happily noted that by 1956 the Port's foreign commerce shipping tonnage had finally recovered to pre-Depression levels — there was one major issue dividing them. In June 1957, the Port Commission unanimously committed itself to pursuing the decades-old dream of dredging a 550-foot-wide and four-mile-long channel up the Duwamish Waterway to provide additional space for industrial development. As the Port began buying parcels of land along the river that summer, lawsuits were filed by opponents who contended that the estimated $23 million cost for the project would ensure that it would remain unprofitable far into the future. While those suits caused a full year of delay, other problems also arose. In November, the tiny riverside town of Tukwila suddenly annexed 1,000 acres within the proposed development area, and the Washington Supreme Court ruled (*Hogue vs. Port of Seattle*) that the Port's actions in condemning land for the project was unconstitutional. The Port was forced to place the Duwamish channel project on the back burner.

CALLS FOR REFORM

By 1957, the Port owned 21 of the 88 piers and terminals on Seattle's waterfront. It was estimated that nearly half the town's annual income originated in harbor-related industries. Yet shipping declined throughout the 1950s. A particularly sore point for Port commissioners was the rate differential certain other ports were granted to compensate for Seattle's geographic advantage. One particularly grating example involved export of Washington apples. The rate advantage granted by federal agencies to the Port of San Francisco allowed it to ship 78,000 boxes of the iconic Washington state fruit in 1954, while a mere 5,480 boxes crossed Seattle's docks.

In addition to coping with government interference, the Port had to deal with a series of reports finding serious fault with the Port during the decade. In 1956, the "Ocean-Borne Commerce of the State of Washington" report, conducted by the University of Washington's Bureau of Business Research for the Port, concluded that, in essence, the Port had failed to remain competitive with other ports. Then, in 1958, a League of Women Voters study documented that ports with governing structures similar to Seattle's typically lacked strong leadership. Compounding such negative analyses was yet another report — this one produced under contract with the Port by the consulting firm Booz, Allen & Hamilton — that reached unflattering conclusions. In addition to noting the obvious — that the commissioners had taken on too many administrative tasks, rather than focusing on their proper role of formulating policy — this study identified another core problem. As historian Padraic Burke wrote: Its "most damaging conclusion was that the Port was an aloof organization, with little contact with the community it served, and without a program of specific goals and objectives." In its recommendations, Booz Allen went on to suggest that the Port's first step should be to meet with a group of responsible community leaders and hash out a realistic set of goals that would benefit the wider community.

This spotlight on problems continued in 1959, when Seattle's NBC affiliate KING-TV aired a documentary, *Lost Cargo*, that chronicled the postwar decline of the Port of Seattle — a general perception supported by the Port's own annual report. Issued in February, it revealed that Seattle's shipping levels had decreased by 15 percent in a year that saw other West Coast ports reporting record gains. The Port clearly had some soul-searching to do. And in July, a newly elected commissioner, Thomas McManus, boldly demanded that all of his fellow commissioners resign — an idea area newspapers seconded on their editorial pages.

Against this backdrop, the election of November 1960 brought passage of two major measures intended to reform and update the Port. Voters approved a proposal, which enjoyed nearly unanimous political support, to expand the Port Commission from three members to five — including two elected at-large. Voters also passed a $10 million Port bond issue that would kick-start a new decade in which Seattle would move from last to first position among West Coast ports in shipping to points east.

TOP: Longshoremen load cargo with pallets and ship's gear, 1950s.

ABOVE: Port of Seattle Annual Report, 1957, showing trade routes.

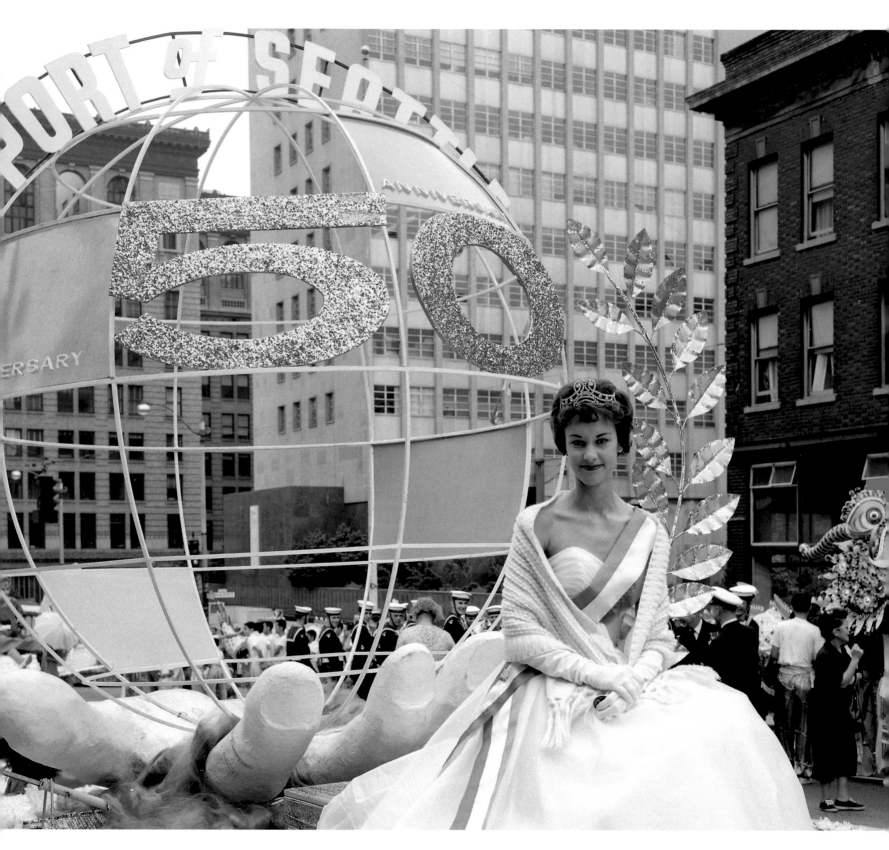

Chapter 5: **REVOLUTION AND RECESSION**

As the Eisenhower Era gave way to President John F. Kennedy's "New Frontier," the Port of Seattle still faced — as did other ports — an era of uncertainty. And the Port, as a string of newspaper editorials pointedly noted, seemed stuck in the past. But this public prodding, combined with internal critiques, soon led to a remarkable turn-around. However, the change was not immediate. The 1960 election of an expanded Port Commission brought first a year of record-breaking maritime trade, followed by almost two years of decline, although this was partly due to personality conflicts on the commission.

POLITICS, PLANNING, AND PROGRESS

This floundering was duly noted by the Washington State Legislature. It held hearings in 1961 to explore the problems at the Port, which led to further reforms that ultimately gave the Port greater taxing authority and power to take the big steps necessary for making the agency more competitive and efficient. Other keys to the Port's subsequent success included implementation of nearly all recommendations of the 1958 Booz, Allen & Hamilton report. These included distancing commissioners from day-to-day operational issues, which

OPPOSITE: Miss Maritime of 1961, Julie Blonk of American Mail Line, showcases the Port's 50th anniversary. For several years, Miss Maritime rode the Port's float in the Maritime Week parades.

resulted in the creation of several departments: Planning and Research, Data Processing, Real Estate, Trade Development, and Public Relations, each staffed by highly regarded professionals.

These changes laid the groundwork for Seattle to be among the first ports to take full advantage of the coming revolution in shipping. For instance, the year 1961 saw the Port reestablish an office in America's heartland. That Chicago outpost was focused on increasing overland business via an emerging advance in the logistics of shipping: the move to containerized cargo. But before a clear path to a successful future could be established, one more breakthrough was needed: the adoption of an initial "Mechanization and Modernization Agreement" between labor and management along the waterfront.

MECHANIZATION AND MODERNIZATION

The emergence of new labor-saving machinery (termed "mechanization") and the application of new work rules requiring greater efficiency (termed "modernization") had been complicating labor-management relations along the waterfront for years. Both ideas had long been resisted by the ILWU, but eventually a Mechanization and Modernization Agreement was hammered out, with the union accepting it in 1960 in exchange for guaranteed hours and no layoffs. The implementation of this agreement ultimately eased the way for Seattle and other Pacific Coast ports to introduce innovations, crucially the concept of shipping goods in standardized containers.

Seattle's waterfront had been one site of early experimentation with containerization. The concept of shipping cargo in reusable, self-contained vans had several direct benefits, including being impervious to pilferage, theft, and water damage. But the key attribute was that the containers could be transferred efficiently from oceangoing vessels to trucks or trains without ever being opened — a great advance for *intermodal* shipping (using multiple modes of transportation — ship, rail, truck — to move freight). However, that very efficiency had negative ramifications for labor. At the time, a team of longshoremen could expect to get four to five days of work in unloading a typical "break-bulk" ship. With containerization, the work could be done in one day, and would require a few newly trained crane operators, rather than many strong-backed men.

CONTAINERIZATION INNOVATION

The roots of containerization extend back at least as far as the 1890s, when European and British railroads began transporting goods in wooden crates. But it took a long time for seagoing operations to follow suit. Finally, in 1929, the Seatrain company began rolling loaded railroad boxcars onto its sea vessels. And then, during World War II, the U.S. military began to transport war materiel in a form of container, which reduced the need for cargo rehandling. After the war, in 1949, Seattle's Alaska Steamship Company innovated a commercially applicable system based on standardized six-foot wooden boxes for use on its regular Seattle-to-Alaska runs out of Pier 42.

But the real breakthrough occurred in the mid-1950s far from Puget Sound, when a North Carolina trucker named Malcolm McLean saw the lingering inefficiencies while waiting impatiently for hours as stevedores unloaded trucks' goods one armload at a time. Over the following years — while his McLean Trucking Co. grew to be the fifth-largest in the country — McLean would continue brainstorming possible solutions to that old dockside bottlenecking problem. In 1955, he sold his interest in McLean Trucking for $5 million and bought the Alabama-based Pan-Atlantic Steamship Company, which he renamed Sea-Land Industries. It was Sea-Land that, in April 1956, became the first trailblazing firm fully dedicated to the revolutionary concept of systematically hauling boxed cargo in stackable metal containers that were loaded aboard the deck of a ship. The practice proved so revolutionary in its efficiency that within one year Sea-Land overtook the dominant shipping firms of the day and vaulted to a leading position in the industry. But beyond that, Mclean was so committed to the concept of global standardization within the industry that he willingly shared his legally protected container-design patents with competitors through a royalty-free lease.

ABOVE: Alaska Steamship Company pioneered its own version of containerization in 1949, starting with eight-by-eight boxes and soon moving to a standard 20-foot container.

OPPOSITE TOP: Longshore union leader Harry Bridges arrives in Seattle via a United flight, 1940s.

BELOW: Alaska Steamship Company's *Chena* in Seattle. The traditional cargo booms and winches soon gave way to designed racks that fit containers.

The Port of Seattle's commissioners were keeping a keen eye on all these developments. As at other ports, Seattle's piers and wharves were geared strictly to traditional break-bulk cargo, and it would require an enormous investment in infrastructure and equipment to change. But, in addition to containers, other big changes were fast approaching — including America's new Interstate Highway system (constructed between 1958 and 1967), which would soon be accessible by coast-to-coast trucking fleets — and Port leaders saw that they needed to fully embrace the future. With containers costing $2,000 or more each, and ships designed to carry them priced at $15 million to $25 million apiece, the costs were significant. These considerations caused certain shipping companies, and most ports, to delay making the expensive changes as long as possible. Portland in particular — because it had captured a great percentage of the West Coast's break-bulk shipping by the early 1960s — was happy with the status quo and failed to make the change that Seattle would. Portland was "unwilling to take the risk of committing the resources it took to speculate on the container business," said Richard D. Ford, executive director of the Port of Seattle from 1977 until 1985. "On the other hand, Seattle had little to lose … It had to take some risk because it was not getting the cargo; it made the decision to speculate on building facilities for containers."

CENTURY 21

In August 1962 — halfway through the six-month run (April 21–October 21) of the town's latest coming-of-age extravaganza, the Century 21 Exposition (or Seattle World's Fair) — the Port announced an ambitious $30 million terminal building program that would reclaim huge tracts of tideland along the Duwamish Waterway to build modern storage and cargo-handling facilities. In addition, the Port would undertake a six-year program to develop marginal lands and sell them to private industry in an effort to broaden Seattle's economic base. These gambles quickly paid off: By the end of the decade, Seattle had vaulted past most of its rivals to become the second-busiest container port on the West Coast.

CRANES AND COMPUTERS

The giant Sea-Land shipping company chose Seattle — specifically, the Port's new Terminal 5 across from Harbor Island on the West Waterway — as its West Coast headquarters in 1964. This partnership was a major coup for the Port, and the town soon had its first of many bright-orange container cranes reaching into the sky.

In an instance of one innovation fostering another, the efficiency of containerization soon begat the first wave of computerization. The speed of containerized freight movement made the traditional paperwork process, which had necessarily bogged down the whole shipping industry, antiquated and obsolete. Hired in 1968 by Port General Manager J. Eldon Opheim, a Port consultant named Clifford C. Muller explained that the "order of magnitude change required the paperwork not to follow the freight but, in fact, for the paperwork to 'drive' the freight. To do that there had to be up-to-the-minute,

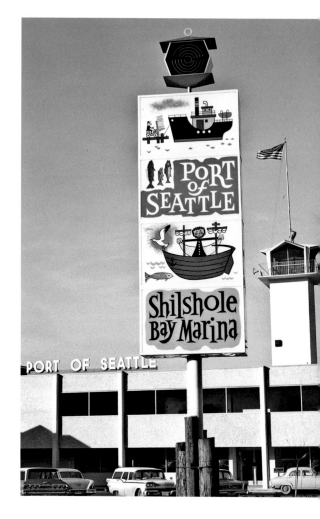

ABOVE: Vintage Shilshole Bay Marina sign, 1963.

OPPOSITE: Over the decades, cargo handling has changed multiple times.

TOP LEFT AND RIGHT: Pallets and wooden boxes give way to cardboard boxes and mechanical gear, 1930s and 1950s.

BELOW LEFT AND RIGHT: Shear-leg derricks and ship's gear once did the work that container cranes do today.

TOP: In 1970, the roads at Sea-Tac were rerouted and parking garage construction began. Sea-Tac was a scene of nonstop activity and construction throughout the decade.

ABOVE: Fighting for equality in construction contracts, Tyree Scott leads a protest at Sea-Tac, 1969.

real-time technology. We put up the first on-line cargo systems in 1969 [and] the first online container system in 1970; and from there implemented the online consolidation system in 1971; and finally warehousing in 1973–74."

In 1970, the Port also inked an agreement with a consortium of six Japanese containership lines — a welcome contract that established Seattle as their "first port of call" and would bring considerable Japanese goods to the West Coast. Thus, the Port's early embrace of containerization and its use of innovative trade techniques gave it a serious head start on other ports, and business boomed once again. Steady increases in trade volume, which had begun in 1963, brought numerous benefits to the region, including the generation of a great number of jobs. The Port's 1971 review of the 1960s notes Seattle harbor tonnage increased 67 percent, from nearly 11 million tons in 1958 to almost 18.4 million tons in 1969. That translated into a 193 percent increase in jobs for truckers, from 210 to 615, and a 240 percent increase in freight service jobs, from 90 to 306. The trend continued throughout the 1970s, when the Northwest experienced little other good economic news.

SEA-TAC EXPANSION: JOBS AND PROTESTS

Construction at Sea-Tac Airport through the 1960s and into the 1970s also generated well-paid jobs for the region, along with some controversy over who would get those jobs. In 1960 and 1961, the Port lengthened Sea-Tac's main runway for the third time, extending it 1,700 feet south via a bridge over South 188th Street, the airport's original boundary. Workers also enlarged the terminal, extending what are now Concourses A and D south and north from the main building, and added more parking, preparing the airport for the more than two million passengers it served in 1962, as Century 21 brought crowds of visitors to town.

By 1966, passenger volume had doubled again, and the airport and its single primary runway were rapidly approaching capacity. Attempting not just to pull even but to leap ahead of the accelerating pace of airline travel, the Port announced in 1967 an ambitious $44 million construction program (the cost would climb to $175 million before it was complete in 1973, driven in part by the high inflation of the early 1970s) to build a second north-south runway and dramatically remake the terminal's aprons and related facilities. The new 9,426-foot runway was located 800 feet west of the existing one. The narrow separation between the runways prevented their simultaneous use during periods with low clouds (some 44 percent of the time), eventually contributing to the need for a third runway.

Work on the second runway was under way in September 1969 when Sea-Tac became the scene of some of the era's more dramatic local civil rights demonstrations. Tyree Scott of the Central Contractors Association led more than 100 protestors onto the

HARBOR ISLAND AND THE DUWAMISH WATERWAYS

HARBOR ISLAND

From ancient times the Duwamish River — whose mouth at Elliott Bay was originally forked by a small cluster of low marshy islands — was the lifeblood of the Duwamish tribe. The river's banks were home for numerous villages; its flowing waters were rich with salmon and herring runs and provided an inland transportation route for canoes. The largest of those estuarial islands was čəqas ("Muddy" or "Something Dirty"), which had long been excellent for deer hunting. In time the soggy land was settled by a chicken rancher named Charles Butler who, failing to file the requisite land-claim paperwork, eventually was forced to vacate.

In 1900, the Seattle General Construction Co. began tideland reclamation by filling the tideflats at the mouth of the river. Then Puget Sound Bridge & Dredging Co. dredged the river to deepen the channel and dumped the spoils onto ceqas, which would become Harbor Island. The firm also used placer-mining technology to sluice soil in large pipes from the Jackson Hill and Dearborn Street regrade projects. After piling up 24 million cubic yards of soil, work was completed in 1909 and the resultant 350-acre area would be, for two decades, the world's largest artificial island.

Harbor Island soon became the home of various private industrial enterprises including the ca. 1911, Fisher Flouring Mills; Associated Shipyards (which constructed steamships during World War I); and Todd Shipyards, which arrived in 1918. In 1926, the Fisher family founded KOMO radio in a broadcasting station behind their mill. In 1933 they acquired Seattle's premier station, KJR, and in 1936 a modern steel radio tower was erected on Harbor Island.

Squeezed for space after the U.S. military took over Seattle's central waterfront during World War II, in 1942 the Port of Seattle purchased the East Waterway Dock on Harbor Island for $900,000. Development of the island continued — in 1967 the Port expanded it to 396 acres — but the years had taken their toll on its environmental health. In 1983, the Environmental Protection Agency — citing tests showing lead-smelting contamination — placed Harbor Island on the National Priority List of polluted sites. The Port decontaminated various areas and continues to monitor the site. Today Harbor Island is home to Todd Pacific Shipyards, a Burlington Northern Santa Fe railyard, several petroleum terminals, and the Port's Piers 16 and 17, the 106-acre Terminal 18 container facility, and Terminals 10 and 102.

WEST WATERWAY

The western bank of the Duwamish River was the site of several traditional villages of the Duwamish peoples, including ha'àh'pus ("Where There Are Horse Clams"), located just north of the Port of Seattle's Terminal 107. The largest one, tuʔəlàlʔtxʷ ("Herring's House"), was at the river's original mouth at Elliott Bay, under today's Spokane Street bridge.

The Port's Terminal 5 is now located on the west bank of the waterway. Decades of unregulated industrial use by Pacific Sound Resources and Lockheed Shipbuilding resulted in the EPA designating the area a Superfund cleanup site. The Port undertook a massive cleanup effort in 1997. Additional expansion of Port facilities on the site spurred the initiation of a multiyear program in June 2008 that led to remediation efforts scheduled to be completed by 2012. Just upstream, the Port runs Terminals 103 and 115, a major barge terminal for goods shipped to Alaska.

EAST WATERWAY

The eastern river bank featured a promontory that was the site of a Duwamish village named tətalxʷqs ("Little Strong Point") that had been used as a defensive refuge. Nearby was a traditional native work station, dəxʷpačəb ("Place For Setting Things Out"). By the 1890s there was a push to excavate a water passageway that would connect Elliott Bay with Lake Washington. While some believed the best route would be via Salmon Bay and Lake Union, others thought cutting through the northern part of Beacon Hill was the answer, and some preferred the Duwamish River. By 1896 Eugene Semple's company had excavated the East Waterway 2,000 feet upstream from Elliott Bay, built bulkheads, and filled in about 50 acres of tidelands — but after much debate, the "South Canal" project was halted in favor of the "North Canal" at Salmon Bay.

During World War II, the Port augmented its Hanford Street Grain Terminal with a major new elevator that in time brought increased business activity. Development continued and today the Port owns Terminals 30, 46, 104, 106, and 108 in this area. Sediments here have been declared a Superfund cleanup site and a multiyear program was initiated in May 2010 that calls for remediation efforts that will be completed sometime after 2013.

LEFT: Postcard view of Fisher Flouring Mills on Harbor Island, 1914.

TOP: Five ships dock at Pier 20, today's Terminal 18, with Seattle's Space Needle in the background, ca. 1970s.

ABOVE: Aerial of Harbor Island and East Waterway, 1967.

airport's flight apron, delaying some flights and shutting down construction. That action and a sit-in at the airport terminal in November were part of a campaign by African American contractors and workers to win a share of federally funded construction projects and jobs ($47 million for Sea-Tac construction came from the federal government). Although the Port and other agencies were amenable, the powerful building trades unions, which largely controlled hiring, resisted calls to open lucrative skilled construction jobs to minorities. Federal District Judge William J. Lindberg prohibited further disruption, but six months later he found the unions in violation of the 1964 Civil Rights Act and imposed a sweeping affirmative action program on the construction industry, including quotas in hiring, training, and union membership. Despite the turmoil, the second runway was completed in September 1970, and work on rebuilding and expanding terminal facilities continued even as the bottom dropped out of the regional economy.

THE BOEING BUST

As the 1960s flowed into the 1970s, the national aerospace industry took a nosedive. Earlier estimates — which projected that the skyrocketing trend-lines of air passenger usage seen between 1955 and 1965 would continue — had been in error. Moreover, since the Northwest region's largest single employer was The Boeing Company, Seattle's economy was hit particularly hard. Just as demand for the 747 model began to slow, the U.S. Congress voted to end its decadelong support for Boeing's supersonic transport (SST) project. Boeing's roster slid from a peak of 100,800 employees in 1967 to a low of 38,690 in April 1971. Whereas Seattle had recently boasted an unemployment rate under the national average, it instantly soared above 12 percent — the highest in the nation and the worst of any major American city since the Great Depression. This recession — known locally as the "Boeing Bust" — saw perhaps 10,000 people moving away to find work. Seattle's problems gained national headlines when two enterprising real-estate agents famously contracted to have a billboard near Sea-Tac Airport display the darkly humorous message: "Will the last person leaving SEATTLE — Turn out the lights?"

Soon after that "sign of the times" garnered national media attention, a new organization formed to counter the notion that Seattle was facing economic collapse. The King County Economic Development Council launched a $2 million advertising campaign designed to play up the good news — and the centerpiece of its message touted the vitality of the Port. But beyond influencing the national audience, this spotlighting of the Port's contributions to the local economy and community also vastly increased the public's knowledge of and appreciation for the Port.

Times had certainly changed. Only 10 years earlier, the Port of Seattle had been, as historian Padraic Burke noted, "scorned and derided as the most backward and crisis-prone port on the West Coast." Now the agency was increasingly seen as a potential savior of the city's future. Boeing began to recover in fits and starts, but it was growth at the Port that helped ease the regional downturn. Among the projects launched during those times was the $25 million purchase of the historic Boeing Plant 1 site — a 25-acre parcel two miles up the Duwamish Waterway that would be developed into a major new facility, Terminal 115. In addition, the old Hanford Street grain elevator was transformed into a large $8 million fully modernized container terminal.

ARCHITECTURE AND ART AT SEA-TAC

Of all the Port projects during the 1970s, it was probably the rebuilding and expansion of Sea-Tac that most affected the public. Work continued steadily, and in July 1973, as air traffic rebounded (5.2 million travelers passed through Sea-Tac that year), the Port unveiled its new terminals and ancillary facilities to general praise. The redevelopment encased the 1949 administration building inside a dramatic new structure featuring vehicle access via an upper drive for departures and a lower level for baggage claim and arrivals. Sky bridges connected the main terminal to a multi-deck parking garage.

Satellite terminals were added north and south of the main building, which passengers reached via a pair of subway loops equipped with driverless automatic shuttle trains. This train was the first of its kind in the nation and opened in 1973 with nine cars. Other improvements included new facilities for fuel, air cargo, and aircraft maintenance. The Port also commissioned $300,000 worth of new works by major local, national, and international artists for the terminal. The unprecedented display — the first of its kind in any U.S. airport — was the beginning of the Port's public art collection, which grew to include significant art works throughout public areas and offices at the airport, in the Port's waterfront headquarters, and at other properties.

ABOVE: Seattle Mayor J. D. Braman greets President Lyndon Johnson at Sea-Tac Airport in 1966.

OPPOSITE TOP LEFT: President John Kennedy visits Seattle on September 27, 1963. Journalists and a crowd of onlookers watch as he walks with Senator Warren Magnuson to a helicopter.

TOP RIGHT: Robert Kennedy addresses a crowd of supporters at Sea-Tac, March 26, 1968.

CHANGING TIMES

Rapidly changing times are unsettling, and the political, economic, and cultural revolutions of the 1960s and '70s were a kaleidoscopic whirlwind. Faced daily with the inescapable evidence of change, the newly buoyant Port was soon hearing from a range of critics. A major emerging issue — especially in the wake of the high-profile nationwide events held on the first annual Earth Day (April 22, 1970) — was the declining state of the environment. Two major points of contention embodied the basic conflict: the issue of noise levels around Sea-Tac Airport and the Port's erection of what was to be the last bulk terminal facility ever built on the Elliott Bay waterfront.

Even before the new Sea-Tac terminal opened, residents in nearby communities were complaining of noise levels caused by increasing jet traffic. Almost 7,000 people petitioned the Port to buy out approximately 2,000 homes in Zone Three, the Federal Aviation Administration–designated area where noise levels were highest. Other residents sued the Port for reduced property value, cracked windows and plaster, and frayed nerves, winning millions in compensation. Seeking a comprehensive solution, the Port and King County — with support and funding from the FAA — began preparing what became known as the Sea-Tac Communities Plan in January 1973. Adopted in 1976, the plan created the nation's first large-scale program to reduce noise impacts by acquiring property outside airport boundaries, as the Port agreed to buy or insulate the homes most affected by aircraft noise. Acquisition proceeded steadily and the Port won several awards for the program, but affected neighbors continued to complain about noise and about the slow pace of insulating their homes.

The controversially massive $13 million Pier 86 Grain Terminal arose bayside in 1970 at the foot of Queen Anne Hill, a long-established neighborhood whose residents treasured their views across Puget Sound. Those views were now marred by a towering industrial edifice that was much more imposing than the original 1967 proposal plans depicted. Other issues included the facility's daily clouds of wafting grain-dust and the loud clanking of railroad cars. Although a public relations problem, the facility was a grand economic success. The modern, automated structure (with a 4.2 million metric ton storage capacity) also boasted a deep-water shipping pier — a pairing that was unmatched on the West Coast.

The new grain terminal was great for Port business but not a big enough factor to quiet critics. Citizen complaints led to hearings in Olympia before the legislature's Committee on Local Government, where a stream of individuals denounced the Port as "aloof" and "unresponsive" to the concerns of local communities. Then, in March 1974, a referendum was held on a proposal to block a project that the Port deemed crucial to marine development on its properties — the financing of a high-rise bridge from I-5 over the Duwamish Waterway to West Seattle. The proposal failed, but it brought about some beneficial soul-searching at the Port. Merle Adlum convinced his fellow commissioners that it was time to commit to being more attuned to community ethics and environmental

ABOVE TOP: A whirly crane rotates and loads containers on a ship at Terminal 46, 1973.

ABOVE: As part of a public access program, the Port opened a fishing pier at Pier 57 in 1968. It was replaced in 1981 by the fishing pier at Terminal 86. The Port now operates 22 parks and public access areas.

OPPOSITE: Seattle waterfront, looking north along the East Waterway, ca. 1965.

Once a cold storage and fish processing site, Terminal 25 became a container terminal occupied by AML, later American President Lines (APL), as shown in this 1976 photo. APL later moved to Terminal 5.

concerns. One example of their heightened sensitivity to such matters was the steps commissioners took to mitigate the Pier 86 grain terminal problems: Pollution controls were added, its grounds were nicely landscaped, and public pedestrian and bicycling paths were installed.

Meanwhile, the challenges the Port faced in balancing its multiple roles in the community were considerable and complicated. It was growth at the Port, after all, that had largely kept the local economy afloat in recent years, and Port leadership knew that it must continue being aggressive to maintain momentum against other ports. Certainly, it was undeniable that competition was heating up again. Although the Port of Seattle had surged ahead of it in the 1960s, the Port of Tacoma succeeded in luring Totem Ocean Trailer Express (TOTE) — a major shipper to Alaska —away from Seattle, partially because the land surrounding the Port of Tacoma was valued at far less than Seattle's and it could easily offer TOTE room to expand. Stung by the loss, the Port of Seattle set out to acquire more than $1.5 million worth of additional land to expand terminals along both sides of the Duwamish Waterway. Other facility enhancements also were planned, including constructing a container freight station at Terminal 25 for APL (one of its biggest carrier customers) and a building for the assembly of imported cars at Terminal 115. The Port also purchased an additional 8.5 acres at Terminal 28, where the Nissan Line would deliver containers and steel — and automobiles. Auto manufacturer Datsun (Nissan)

ABOVE: Imported cars at Terminal 91, 1982. Tens of thousands of cars entered the U.S. through Seattle during the 1970s and 1980s.

LEFT: The *Liu Lin Hai*, the first Chinese ship to enter a U.S. port in 30 years, loads grain at Terminal 86 in April 1979. A public pathway runs beside the Terminal 86 Grain Facility.

declared Seattle its "point of entry" for automobiles destined for the Midwestern and East Coast markets. (Terminals 25 and 28 have since been incorporated into Terminal 30.)

In 1975 — in a sort of one-step-back, two steps-forward shuffle — longtime Port user United Brands suddenly announced that it would end four decades of making weekly banana boat calls, opting instead to transport its product via rail and trucks. But that same year, the Japan Six-Line shipping consortium added vessels that doubled its container capacity, and the Port offered the firm use of Terminal 37 at decade's end. Then in 1976 the Port reacquired the 198-acre Terminal 91 facility (Piers 90 and 91 at Smith

ABOVE: The captain and officers of the *Liu Lin Hai* disembark at Terminal 91, April 18, 1979.

RIGHT: Port Commissioner Jack Block peers over the shoulder of Commissioner Henry Kotkins (second from right) to join Senator Henry Jackson (center), Chinese officials, and the captain of the *Liu Lin Hai* in celebrating the ship's arrival in Seattle, April 18, 1979.

Cove) from the U.S. Navy and subsequently devoted it to cold storage for seafood exports to Japan and other Asian markets.

Another international breakthrough occurred in 1979 when President Jimmy Carter's administration announced the opening of full diplomatic ties with the People's Republic of China — a move long advocated by U.S. Senator Warren G. Magnuson of Washington. That April, maritime history was made when a Chinese-owned cargo ship — the *Liu Lin Hai* — cruised into Puget Sound and docked at Pier 91. The 637-foot, Norwegian-built ship brought no cargo, but it left Seattle with 37,000 metric tons of corn from the Midwest that it loaded at the Pier 86 grain terminal. The historic event ended a 30-year trade embargo and established Seattle as the first U.S. port to host a vessel from the country that would eventually become the Port's largest import trade partner.

Following the end of the Vietnam War in 1975, there was further evolution in Asian trade markets, and the Port of Seattle was among the first to send trade representatives to Vietnam to discuss opportunities. But at the same time, a new business model was emerging for imported goods that placed a premium on how close a harbor was to population centers where cargo could be sold. Under this model, Seattle's efficiency as a hub of intermodal transport was no longer as persuasive as it once had been. Instead, emerging Asian exporters were powerfully attracted to the idea of shipping to the ports of Los Angeles and Long Beach, which offered not only an immediate market of 7 million consumers for their goods, but also train and truck connections to the rest of the country. King County's population of 1.1 million simply could not compete with Southern California.

A significant parallel development was under way, as the Carter administration persuaded Congress in 1978 to deregulate the airline industry, allowing carriers to determine their own domestic routes and fares. Airlines strongly supported deregulation, but many were unprepared for the resulting price wars and unfettered competition, particularly since the change came in the midst of a nationwide recession that crimped air travel and put economic pressure on carriers. Plenty of new airlines sprang up, but a lot of them, along with some industry stalwarts, soon went bankrupt. Airline workers also took a hit, as financially squeezed companies pressured unions to sacrifice wages and benefits or see their jobs disappear. In the long run, both the number of airlines serving Sea-Tac and the number of passengers would reach new highs, but passenger traffic, which had reached nearly 10 million in 1979, dropped sharply over the next two years.

A new era was dawning that would at once challenge the Port of Seattle to reinvent itself yet again and cause the people of Seattle to reimagine their beloved town and begin planning for its rapid emergence as a truly world-class city.

LEFT: Air cargo through Sea-Tac has increased annually since 1955. Here, a China Airlines aircraft is loaded, 1980.

ABOVE: Special supplement published in community newspapers in July 1973, celebrating Sea-Tac Airport's 25th anniversary.

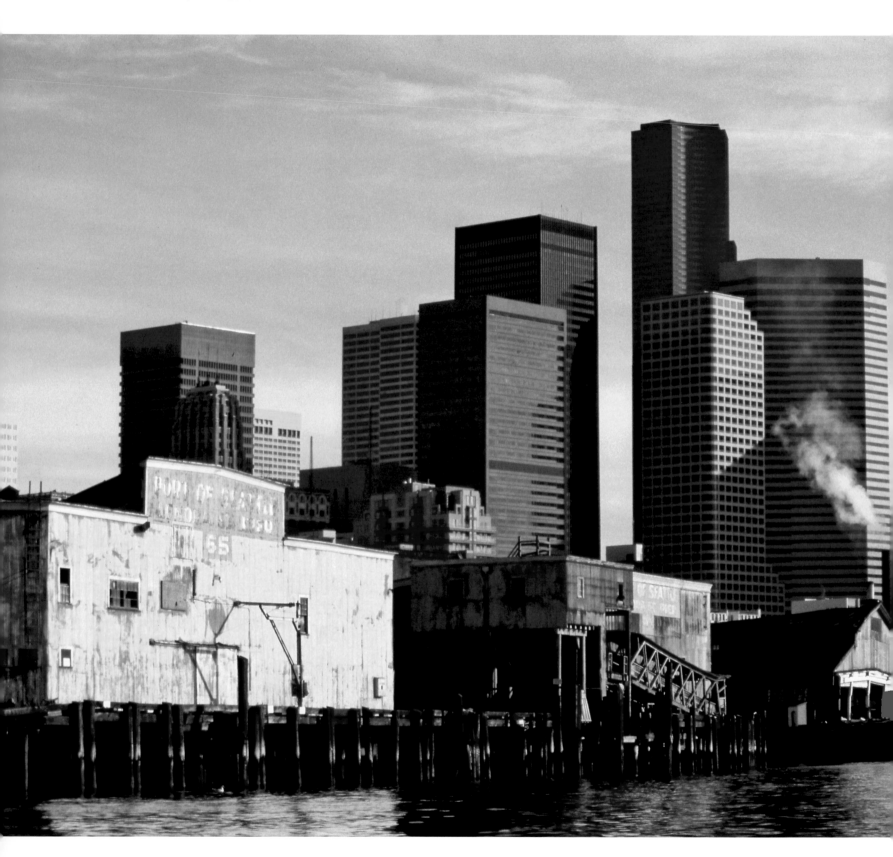

Chapter 6: **COMPETITION AND EXPANSION**

The sluggish global economy of the 1970s had presented significant hurdles to the leaders of many industries — including interconnected ones, such as ports, steamship lines, railroads, trucking companies, and airlines. However, due in great measure to the leadership at the Port of Seattle, which had kept its eyes on the prize — the rapidly modernizing economies of various Asian countries — the Pacific Northwest suffered less than some areas. And when the Pacific Rim boom erupted in full force during the 1980s, careful preparations had positioned Seattle to capitalize on the increased trade. A visionary concept took hold that saw Seattle as a "crossroads" city strategically located between Asia and Europe.

OPPOSITE: The derelict condition of the central waterfront, shown in 1986, led the Port to embark on a major redevelopment and revival of the area.

BUILDING A WORLD-CLASS CITY

Piers 64, 65, and 66 were torn down to make room for the first of the central waterfront redevelopment projects, the new Bell Street Pier, 1995.

The notion that it was Seattle's rightful destiny to be recognized as a world-class city was long held by many residents and business leaders. The Port would be instrumental in achieving that goal by sparking general business growth, which would attract the waves of incoming population required for a metropolis to reach critical mass. It took the creative contributions of many individuals and companies to turn the dream into reality.

Innovative new local companies, such as Microsoft and Starbucks, joined forces with such established heavyweights as Boeing, Weyerhaeuser, and PACCAR to help catapult Seattle into the big leagues. Improved attractions along the central waterfront, major-league sports, and the arts also helped. Real estate values soared, investors and developers bought in, and the city's skyline was quickly altered with scores of new high-rise office and residential buildings. Perhaps the most visible change fostered by the Port during the 1980s was along Seattle's central waterfront. An area decades in decline, the waterfront was about to see a major upgrade — in both public amenities and harbor

AIR CARGO AT SEA-TAC

From their earliest days, airplanes have carried goods as well as people. Indeed cargo — specifically United States mail — played a critical role in the development of both commercial airplanes and passenger airlines. The Boeing Company got its start building warplanes for the U.S. military during World War I, but when the war ended the new company nearly went broke — until Boeing test pilot Eddie Hubbard demonstrated the viability of transporting mail by air when he and Bill Boeing flew to Canada and returned with America's first international airmail delivery. Within months the U.S. Post Office (now the Postal Service) began granting contracts for scheduled airmail service to private companies, many flying Boeing planes. Air travel grew as more and more passengers rode on the mail planes and Boeing went on to develop powerful new planes. At Hubbard's urging, Boeing also bid for and won the Post Office's lucrative Chicago to San Francisco mail route. The air transport unit that Boeing created to serve the route grew into airline behemoth United Air Lines.

By the time Seattle-Tacoma International Airport was dedicated in 1949, United and the other airlines serving it concentrated largely on passenger service, carrying a relatively small amount of mail and other cargo (just over 6,000 tons in 1950, Sea-Tac's first full year of operation) in the bellies of their passenger liners. Sea-Tac's first cargo-only carrier — Flying Tiger Line, many of whose pilots had "flown the hump" ferrying troops and supplies over the Himalayas during World War II — arrived in 1952. Mail was still a big part of air cargo, and just as the Post Office had earlier given Boeing and United a leg up, it helped boost Sea-Tac's cargo business by designating it in 1956 as the airport for shipping all first-class mail to Asia from west of the Mississippi. The Post Office airmail facility built the next year saw huge increases in airmail from Sea-Tac to Southeast Asia as U.S. involvement in the Vietnam War increased. Total air cargo rose to 48,660 tons in 1964, doubled to 96,437 tons in 1967, and jumped another 30 percent to 123,577 tons in 1968.

Airmail volume dropped sharply as the Vietnam War wound down and the airmail center was eventually moved to San Francisco, bringing temporary declines in total cargo shipped through Sea-Tac. However, other types of air cargo

continued to grow. During the 1960s, high quality, low weight freight and highly perishable items were increasingly carried in the bellies of passenger planes. In addition, by the early 1970s, two more cargo-only carriers joined Flying Tiger (which was later purchased by FedEx). The Port added air cargo facilities during the 1970s and then doubled cargo-handling capacity in the early 1980s with a new air cargo center. The Port's Sea-Air cargo program — container ships from Asia seamlessly unloaded cargo onto trucks that rushed it to airplanes at Sea-Tac for immediate flight onward to European markets — proved particularly successful. In 1990, Sea-Tac ranked first worldwide in volume of sea-air cargo.

Today more than a quarter-million tons of air cargo passes through Sea-Tac every year. Seven freighter carriers serve the airport (Alaska Air Cargo, Cargolux, China Airlines Cargo, EVA Air Cargo, FedEx Express Freight, Korean Air Cargo, and Martinair Cargo) while more than 20 airlines carry cargo on their passenger jets. Among the wide variety of cargos are some iconic representatives of the region Sea-Tac serves. Since 1984, when Northwest Orient Airlines carried the first shipment of local cherries to South Korea, Sea-Tac exports jump dramatically each summer as 25 to 30 million pounds of fresh Washington cherries are shipped to Korea and Taiwan for distribution throughout Asia. Another unique Washington food — the geoduck — is also hugely popular in Asia, with 15 to 20 thousand pounds shipped through Sea-Tac each season. Spare parts for Washington-made Boeing planes are also part of Sea-Tac's air cargo — since it opened in 1993, Boeing's Spares Distribution Center has shipped millions of parts to customers around the world, keeping the global aircraft fleet aloft.

FROM TOP: Flying Tiger Air Cargo, 1970s; Loading logs at Sea-Tac; 1985. Northwest cherries destined for China, 2001; Alaska Air Cargo, 2010.

ABOVE TOP: Cappy Thompson's stained glass window, *I Was Dreaming of Spirit Animals*, installed in Concourse A in 2004. In 1969, the Port dedicated $300,000 for art at Sea-Tac, and the airport now features more than 100 works by 59 regional and internationally recognized artists.

ABOVE: Double-stacked rail cars doubled the amount of cargo a train could carry. These new cars were introduced in the mid-1980s.

OPPOSITE TOP: In 1983, businessman and local personality Ivar Haglund (of Ivar's Seafood Restaurants) ran for Port Commission as a publicity stunt. To his surprise, he was elected and held the seat from 1984 to 1985.

BELOW: Loading wheat seed, 1984.

facilities. Throughout the 1980s, the Port invested an unprecedented $512 million in a massive modernization and expansion program.

CONTAINERIZATION (PART 2) AND COMPETITION

Thanks to the foresight of Port leadership, the second containerization revolution, sparked by the railroad industry, paid long-lasting dividends to the local economy. The railroads had come to realize they could double the number of containers hauled on their flatcars simply by stacking the metal boxes two-high. This novel idea, while providing remarkable gains in efficiency, also required expensive design changes to containers, along with the reconstruction of many bridges, crossings, and other facilities to make room for the higher loads (some, like the Stampede Pass tunnel in the Cascade mountain range, have yet to be enlarged). The Port itself needed to invest considerable sums in converting its terminals to accommodate these changes.

Another major development came in the 1980s, when one of the world's largest shipping firms, APL (formerly called American President Lines Ltd.), commissioned the construction of $100 million C-10 vessels, which, as a class, became known as "post-Panamax" ships. The name derived from the fact that for decades most oceangoing freighters had been limited to less that 1,000 feet long and 91 feet wide — dimensions imposed by the physical limits of the Panama Canal locks. Now, with railroads and trucking providing efficient transcontinental transport for most goods, APL instead committed to building giant ships that couldn't pass through the Canal, but, by carrying up to 30 percent more cargo, would work well on the lucrative trans-Pacific trade routes.

At the same time, competition sharpened with other ports, both distant and near. Having embraced containerization later than Seattle, the Port of Tacoma aggressively marketed its new container and dockside intermodal facilities in the 1980s, including on-dock rail spurs that allowed loading of containers directly onto flatcars. Sea-Land became the first of several container lines to move operations from Seattle to Tacoma. Later, Tacoma also lured away former Port of Seattle customers K-Line and Evergreen Marine Corp. of Taiwan. This keen competition — and the perception that shipping lines were playing the ports against each other — led to increasing calls to merge the two Puget Sound ports or create a state port authority, potential solutions that have yet to gain traction.

Despite such competition, the Port of Seattle continued to grow and to foster regional economic development. But the role of the agency had evolved to such an extent that Port leadership realized the larger community had a diminished sense of what the Port actually *did*. No longer just the destination or transshipment point it had been in earlier years, the Port was, in essence, now a landlord and a builder of transportation infrastructure, and that was harder to package in an easily understood concept. So, as the

Port's role evolved, its leaders thought the public no longer fully understood or necessarily supported desired initiatives. Perhaps that helps explain why on November 8, 1983, area voters elected to the Seattle Port Commission a candidate whose whole campaign amounted to a publicity gag: the local seafood restaurateur and celebrity Ivar Haglund.

THE PACIFIC RIM

Business was booming. After the call of the *Liu Lin Hai*, a massive new market opened for the Port of Seattle. In 1980, a delegation headed by Lin Zuyi from the China Ocean Shipping Company (COSCO) arrived and began forging a relationship with the Port. Soon thereafter, the Port of Shanghai sent four managers to participate in a three-month training internship at the Port, and upon their return, they set out to successfully develop China's first container terminal at the Port of Shanghai. From there, the business interactions between the two nations grew splendidly: A U.S.–China trade level of only $4.81 billion in 1980 soared to $366 billion two decades later.

The 1980s also made intermodal connections increasingly important — particularly dockside rail lines — and the Port's efforts to accommodate demand paid off. During that decade, Seattle's waterfront saw further development and ever-higher shipping activity. Companies central to this growth included China Ocean Shipping Co. (which nearly doubled its capacity by adding two more dedicated ships); Evergreen (which increased its activity by 40 percent); Hanjin Shipping Co. of South Korea (which added larger vessels to increase capacity by 40 percent); and U.S.–based Matson Navigation Co. (which doubled its capacity).

By decade's end, the Port was handling more than 1 million containers per year. And with labor and management committed to working more closely together, a new record for container crane productivity was set in 1989. In some cases, the growth in traffic was a direct result of the Port providing improved marine facilities to help ensure the competitive position of its customers. For example, in 1985, the Port completed one of its crown jewels: a $12 million expansion of its Terminal 106 national distribution center (which was followed in 1986 by another $9 million augmentation). This facility became the successful home for one of the world's largest toy manufacturing companies, Hasbro Inc., which made Seattle its sole port of entry for containerized shipments from Asia.

Similarly, when videogame maker Nintendo Co. Ltd. of Kyoto, Japan, moved its U.S. operations (Nintendo of America, Inc.) from New York City to King County (Redmond, Washington) in 1982, the company cited the area's transportation and Port facilities as contributing to its decision. Other advances at the Port included the investment of $50 million in redeveloping the

ABOVE: Terminal 46 as it appeared in 1983.

OPPOSITE TOP LEFT: Another expansion of the parking garage at Sea-Tac, now the largest parking garage under one roof in North America, 1992.

TOP RIGHT: Staff monitor the airport Satellite Transit System 24 hours a day, 1982.

BELOW: 1985 Annual Report

77-acre Terminal 5 facility. The Port also invested $3.9 million in preparing Terminal 25 for Matson, and improved and expanded Terminal 30 with additional acreage, new buildings, and the installation of three 100-foot-gauge container cranes. Terminal 42 was augmented with a new state-of-the-art computerized gatehouse to increase the efficiency of container movement through the facility.

The Port had to pull out all the stops to keep APL, one of its anchor tenants, which wanted a new "super terminal." APL was not only the largest container carrier serving exclusively the Pacific Basin, it also accounted for at least 20 percent of Seattle harbor shipping volume. So, when the company put out a request for proposals to the ports of Tacoma, Oakland, and Los Angeles/Long Beach, the Port of Seattle worked with the mayor, city council, local business leaders and labor representatives, and various state and federal agencies to cobble together a winning plan. In the end, the Port of Seattle prevailed, Terminal 5 was expanded to APL's approval, and a great number of local jobs were saved. But APL wasn't the only shipping firm seeking more and better intermodal operations, and the Port invested $3.5 million in a new on-dock rail yard at Terminal 18. By 1990, the agency was conducting trade business worth more than $26 billion with 125 countries and was able to boast that its facilities offered Port customers "more intermodal choices than any other West Coast port."

SEA-TAC UPGRADES

Just as marine cargo volumes grew, aviation businesses were on the rise. In the early 1980s, a new air cargo center doubled Sea-Tac's cargo-handling capacity. Passenger air traffic also began climbing again. There were more new nonstop routes to Asian and European destinations. But it was the remarkable growth in feeder air service between Seattle and other Northwest cities that led to the explosive rise in airport passenger numbers. During this time, Sea-Tac's commuter/regional aircraft operations more than tripled, from 41,747 in 1978 to 150,376 in 1990. Smaller carriers like Horizon and United Express provided frequent service from Sea-Tac to Spokane, Yakima, Walla Walla, Portland, Boise, and other regional destinations, at fares low enough to compete with auto travel. In 1985, before Horizon arrived, 20-year projections showed no need for a third runway. Three years later, traffic had already reached levels predicted for 2005, and Port and regional planners concluded that a third runway to allow two arrival streams in all weather was required to meet the region's future air capacity needs.

Nine years of further planning, studies, public comment, and controversy followed before the Port Commission, on May 27, 1997, adopted the final version of a master plan including the third runway, which then was approved by the Federal Aviation Administration on July 3. Many who lived near Sea-Tac vociferously opposed another runway, and the Airport Communities Coalition, which included the cities of Burien, Des Moines, Federal Way, Normandy Park, and Tukwila, and the Highline School District, filed numerous appeals challenging the project; litigation continued for years.

During the long process of studying the new runway, the Port also was making improvements to terminals and other airport facilities. Having spent $40 million in 1985 to upgrade the airport with new gates, the Port completed a more ambitious $167 million program of improvements in 1992, a year in which Sea-Tac served nearly 18 million passengers. The project, dubbed "First Class Upgrade," added 3,500 parking spaces in the garage as well as new short-term parking, renovated concourses, and added more gates. With the help of federal funding, the Port also installed new surface detection radar and lighting to increase the capacity and safety of runways and taxiways during low-visibility conditions.

FEDERAL DEREGULATION AND FTZ EXPANSION

The decades of the 1980s and 1990s brought major changes on the political and governmental fronts, with the deregulation of big business continuing apace. The effects on the Port and related industries were significant. For example: the trucking and rail industries

ABOVE LEFT: Dedication of the public fishing pier at Terminal 86, 1981.

ABOVE RIGHT: In 1986, Northwest apples are readied for export to the Middle East at Terminal 91, then the West Coast's largest cold storage facility. The facility was later converted to commercial fishing industry use.

OPPOSITE TOP: Program of events celebrating 100 years of trade with Japan and the Nippon Yusen Kaisha (NYK) shipping line in 1996.

BOTTOM: Vessel *Asian Venture* at Terminal 30, 1991.

suddenly were given the right to enter and leave markets — a new factor that encouraged competition but also increased uncertainty. In addition, shipping rates would no longer be set by rate bureaus, but negotiated in the open marketplace. Rather than simplifying matters, such regulatory changes seemed to lead quickly to chaotic pricing systems with little stability. The Port responded in 1981 by establishing its own Truck Contract Program to simplify and stabilize prices, and it provided additional services the industry had long needed. The plan was expanded and improved over time, and shippers were pleased to have access to a menu of intermodal transportation options.

In 1989, the Foreign Trade Zone Board granted Seattle the opportunity to radically expand the Port's previously puny 1.4-acre site on Harbor Island. The variety of services the Port could now offer potential customers was greatly augmented when Foreign Trade Zone status was conferred on 1,400 acres of the agency's properties — virtually all of its seaport and airport facilities.

NAFTA AND INTERNATIONALISM

That same year, Congress approved a bilateral Canada–United States Free Trade Agreement, and by the 1992 presidential election, the expanded North American Free Trade Agreement (NAFTA), which now embraced Mexico, had become controversial. While some were, and remain, concerned about potential job losses, others were bullish on the idea of vastly increased business opportunities. For its part, the Port stepped up to help form the Trade Development Alliance of Greater Seattle in support of such international policies and the business it believed would be generated (the alliance also included representatives of King County, the City of Seattle, the Seattle Chamber of Commerce, and union leaders). One immediate boost for Seattle was being named by *Fortune* magazine the "best city for global business in the U.S."

The Port was certainly doing its part to nourish that reputation. In 1992, in collaboration with the state and the Port of Tacoma, the Port established the only state-sponsored trade office in Paris. That same year, Russia — which had experienced the political collapse of the Soviet Union in December 1991 — chose Seattle for a new consulate, and the new government and the Port exchanged fact-finding missions. In 1994, the ports of Seattle and Tacoma supported the opening of a Washington State Trade Office in Vladivostok. Taking it a step further, the Port established a partnership with Seattle–King County Convention and Visitors Bureau and the state to promote tourism from markets that offer direct flights to Seattle.

That year, another Port investment paid off in a big way. The prior year, it had invested $10.4 million to triple the capacity of cold storage warehouse space at Terminal 91 to accommodate the growing apple trade. That creation of what was the West Coast's largest on-dock refrigerated storage was timed perfectly, because Japan finally lifted its 23-year ban on Washington fruit imports. Improved facilities, better marketing, and increased international outreach all worked wonders, and by 1996, the ports of Seattle and Tacoma, local rivalry notwithstanding, combined to handle a higher container volume than anywhere else in the United States except Los Angeles/Long Beach, and to handle more trade between New York and Asia than passed through New York Harbor.

THE ENVIRONMENT

Far more than in earlier years, Port growth and development included attention to environmental issues. In the 1970s, Sea-Tac become the first airport in the nation to employ a full-time wildlife biologist to control species that could be hazardous to air traffic and to promote the conservation of others. Habitat restoration projects, frequently in conjunction with other local, state, and federal agencies, were carried out as part of new marine terminal construction on the Duwamish Waterway.

In the 1980s, the Port agreed in principle to purchase the former Lockheed shipyard, a huge plot of land just north of Terminal 5 that held promise for expansion of the Port's container facilities. In keeping with its increased focus on environmental questions, the Port made the deal contingent upon Lockheed's completing both an environmental study and cleanup of the upland area, while the Port undertook a study of the underwater acreage.

During that same period, the Port engaged a new Neighbors Advisory Committee comprising nearby Magnolia and Queen Anne residents to discuss issues surrounding Terminal 91. The collaboration resulted in improvements that included the T-91 Bike Trail. Similar cooperative efforts with other community groups and city officials produced a comprehensive public access plan for the Duwamish Waterway.

CENTRAL WATERFRONT REDEVELOPMENT

While other areas of the Port were being revitalized, Seattle's central waterfront was becoming increasingly derelict. The old Railroad Avenue had been a confusing and dangerous tangle of tracks, docks, and maritime commerce; three quarters of a century later, the problem was not too much activity on the street, now called Alaskan Way, but too little. With almost all cargo being handled at the Port's modern container terminals south of downtown, only three of 16 central waterfront piers still housed maritime uses; Piers 64 and 65 sat vacant and cordoned off with barbed wire and no-trespassing signs. Along the other piers were empty, decaying sheds, T-shirt vendors, and tacky tourist shops, while small warehouses and weedy vacant lots lined the east side of the street under the steep bluff leading up to downtown. Calling the waterfront a "virtual no man's land," several citizen groups pushed for change.

In response, the Port began in the mid-1980s to shape the Central Waterfront Project. Helping guide the idea to reality were the first two women to serve on the Port Commission — Patricia "Pat" Davis, elected in 1986, and Paige Miller, who joined her two years later. The women shared a background as community activists and, with their participation, the commission began displaying increased sensitivity to community impacts, ranging from airport noise to the state of the historic waterfront.

The Port began by relocating its headquarters from the Bell Street Pier (Pier 66) site it had occupied since 1915 to a stylish building on Pier 69 (at the foot of Clay Street) — the former site of the Roslyn Coal & Coke Company facility built in 1900. Several years later, New York's American Can

MIC DINSMORE

In June 1992, Mic Dinsmore became the Port's new executive director, and would go on to serve for almost 15 years, longer than any other executive in Port history.

Raised in the mining town of Butte, Montana, he was characterized as ambitious and tough-minded. He served as the Port's Marine Division director from 1985 to 1988, tasked with increasing container cargo volumes and initiating the planning for long-range harbor development. For two years he served as chief operating officer, responsible for day-to-day operations of the Aviation, Marine, Logistics and Administrative divisions.

During his tenure as chief executive, he would oversee several major capital projects. Completion of the Central Waterfront Project was one of his first priorities. Other projects included the construction of the new Concourse A, Central Terminal, and the third runway at Sea-Tac Airport, and renovation or development of four container terminals and two cruise terminals.

Despite considerable achievements, he faced criticism for a management style that some characterized as aggressive or domineering, and controversy over contracting policies and other issues. He retired as CEO in March 2007.

Company moved in and made good use of the facility's spacious 301-foot-by-60-foot dock and two-story warehouse for many years. Thoroughly refurbished by the Port, today the building houses the Port headquarters as well as a terminal for the high-speed Victoria Clipper catamaran ferries and other tenants. Port offices were dedicated in March 1993.

The headquarters move cleared the way for the Port to develop the former site of Piers 64, 65, and 66 into the centerpiece of the new central waterfront. The new Bell Street Pier, completed in 1996, featured 11 acres of public waterfront with plazas (including a rooftop park where the first Port Commission had established a park 80 years prior), a fountain, restaurants, and the Bell Harbor Marina, downtown's only recreational marina, with room for 70 boats. Across the street, work got under way on the Waterfront Landing Condominiums, the first residences on the central waterfront since tribal camps and fishermen's shanties were displaced from that exact spot by railroad tunnel construction and regrades in the years before the Port's formation.

The plazas, restaurants, marina, and condos were just the start. Development continued on both sides of Alaskan Way, and in the new century, Bell Street Pier would be the scene of a fast-growing, economy-boosting maritime business.

ABOVE: From the Pier 66 rooftop, Port of Seattle CEO Mic Dinsmore welcomes the cruise business: "Seattle is a first-class tourism destination with first class facilities that can support the newest and largest cruise ships."

OPPOSITE: The new Bell Street Pier, completed in 1996, featured 11 acres of public waterfront with plazas, a fountain, restaurants, and the Bell Harbor Marina. A fully operational cruise terminal opened in 2000.

Chapter 7: GREEN GATEWAY

The FAA granted final approval in July 1997 for the third runway at Seattle-Tacoma International Airport. Preliminary work began soon thereafter, but construction was delayed several times by the Airport Communities Coalition's pending legal challenges; another decade would pass before the runway opened. As the first work began on the runway, one of the final components of the Port's central waterfront development was being completed. The World Trade Center complex opened in October 1998 across Alaskan Way from the Bell Harbor Marina and Conference Center at Pier 66. The complex comprised two commercial office towers and a Port-owned building housing trade organizations and providing a venue for trade and business development meetings. The new World Trade Center was one of the venues where the World Trade Organization (WTO) met in Seattle in late 1999. Port commissioners joined with city and state officials to welcome the WTO conference as an opportunity to showcase the region's trade prospects on an international stage, but things did not turn out quite as planned.

OPPOSITE: Opened in May 2005, Sea-Tac's Central Terminal once again gives passengers a dramatic view of the airfield. This new 240,000 square-foot "heart of the airport" has seating and tables for 500 travelers and is encircled by more than 40,000 square feet of concessions.

Norwegian Star moors at Bell Street Pier
Cruise Terminal, 2006. In 2010, six cruise lines
homeported 11 ships in Seattle, with weekly
sailings to Alaska.

As the new millennium began, the Port took major steps toward developing the shoreside infrastructure for a form of maritime commerce that had not been significant in the region for many years: luxury cruise ships. In 1999, only six cruise ships called in Seattle. The next year, the first phase of the Port's Bell Street Pier Cruise Terminal was completed and regularly scheduled cruise service began. In 2000, Seattle became homeport to ships from Norwegian Cruise Line and Royal Caribbean International, and total cruise ship calls increased to 36. That was just the beginning: Phase Two of the Bell Street Terminal was completed in 2001, and the numbers of ship calls and passengers continued to grow through the decade, generating thousands of jobs and pumping nearly $2 million per homeport ship call into the regional economy. The rapid growth in cruise ship traffic also raised concerns over water and air pollution that the Port had to address.

In February 2001, the Nisqually earthquake shattered the control tower at Sea-Tac and damaged airport offices and some marine terminals, requiring significant repair work. Then the deadly terrorist attacks of September 11, 2001, brought air travel to a temporary, shocked standstill. At the Port of Seattle, like all agencies responsible for airports, seaports, and other vulnerable transportation infrastructure, the 9/11 attacks

TWO INTERNATIONAL TRADE CONFERENCES, TWO DIFFERENT OUTCOMES

Establishing and maintaining strong trade relationships is critical for Washington, where one in three jobs is dependent on trade. In recent decades the Port of Seattle has been a leader on this front, and helped host trade conferences that drew trade ministers and heads of state from across the globe.

APEC 1993

In November 1993, Seattle hosted the Asia-Pacific Economic Cooperation (APEC) conference, highlighting the region and its burgeoning prospects for international trade. President Bill Clinton drew global attention to the meeting when he invited leaders of the other Pacific Rim APEC nations to join him at the annual conference, usually only attended by lower-level officials. Clinton presided at a trade summit in the Native American-style long house at Blake Island State Park, a short boat ride from the Seattle waterfront, with Chinese President Jiang Zemin, Japanese Prime Minister Morihiro Hosokawa, and 11 other heads of state.

More than 3,000 reporters covered the talks, giving Seattle invaluable exposure on the international stage. The weeklong conference established what Clinton called a "framework of cooperation" as participants worked to liberalize international trade and investment by reducing regulations affecting them — a goal that then seemed relatively uncontroversial. Writing two years later, author Dick Paetzke suggested that for some, "this prestigious event established that Seattle has bright prospects as a new Geneva, an international crossroads where government, enterprise and people of good will can meet to work things out in concord."

Things did not always work out that way: Despite APEC's accomplishments, concord proved harder to find when the WTO met in Seattle six years later.

WTO 1999

Delegates from the 135 member countries of the World Trade Organization (WTO) met at the Washington State Convention & Trade Center from November 30 to December 3, 1999, intending to finalize an agenda for further expansion of international trade. From the outset there was little agreement in the convention center or on the streets, and the ensuing "battle in Seattle" did nothing to boost either prospects for trade or the city's image.

With major corporations like Boeing, Microsoft, and Weyerhaeuser, the state's large agricultural sector, and numerous small businesses all heavily dependent on international markets, there was strong support for the WTO and its efforts to reduce trade barriers. Port Commissioner

Patricia Davis, the president of the nonprofit Washington Council on International Trade, initiated the successful effort to host the WTO with strong support from her former commission colleague, Seattle Mayor Paul Schell, Washington Governor Gary Locke, Boeing CEO Phil Condit, Microsoft CEO Bill Gates, and many other organizations, elected officials and businesses.

Though labor unions and some environmental groups participating on the steering committee disagreed with the WTO's agenda, they nevertheless backed the plan to host the meeting. Many groups with deep roots in the region condemned the WTO for favoring corporate interests over social and environmental concerns. Even the longshore workers from Seattle's ILWU Local 19, despite the trade-dependent nature of their own jobs, joined fellow union members to march against the WTO on the conference's opening day, November 30, 1999.

Seattle authorities responsible for security appeared completely unprepared for the huge crowds of protestors that filled downtown early that morning, when thousands of nonviolent protestors accomplished their well-publicized goal by temporarily shutting down the WTO, forcing cancellation of opening ceremonies. An estimated 50,000 protestors organized by the AFL-CIO made the anti-WTO protest one of the largest in Seattle's history. A group of 100 or fewer smashed windows and sprayed graffiti. Police responded with a massive show of force, turned much of the retail core into a "no protest zone" for the duration of the conference, and arrested hundreds there the next day.

The conference ended without reaching the agreement it had been called to achieve because of two insurmountable hurdles—protective farm policies in Europe, Japan and the U.S., and unfair trade practices between wealthy industrialized nations and smaller, less-developed countries. The WTO continues to try to resolve these issues.

While some felt the protests and police response may have tarnished the City of Seattle's image, the Port of Seattle's ongoing interest in trade development activity has firmly established it as an influential voice on international trade.

ABOVE: President Bill Clinton joins Port Commissioner Patricia Davis, right, at a presentation on international trade during the WTO convention, 1999.

were quickly followed by major new security initiatives. Changes in security measures were most visible to the public in the passenger screening lines at the airport, but over the next several years, significant changes and new expenditures were required at both the airport and seaport. Design for the expansion of Sea-Tac's passenger terminal, in progress since 1996, was revised to accommodate new security procedures and screening equipment, adding to the cost of the project. Enhancing security across the sprawling seaport facilities posed different challenges. In the years following 9/11, the Port spent millions, much of it provided by federal security grants, to increase security staffing, add lighting, and upgrade perimeter security at waterfront terminals, and to work with origination ports to increase security at the start of the supply chain. Nevertheless, only a fraction of containers could be inspected at either end, worrying critics, who called for even tougher measures.

The rise of security concerns had one silver lining for the Port: The greater number of Americans choosing to vacation nearer home boosted the domestic cruise ship industry. With Alaska a top domestic cruise destination, the trend accelerated Seattle's rapid growth as a cruise-ship homeport. By 2003, two more cruise lines, Holland America Line and Princess Cruises, were sailing from Elliott Bay to Alaska. To accommodate them, the Port quickly opened a second, temporary cruise terminal just south of downtown at Terminal 30, vacated by container lines that had shifted operations to Terminal 5.

As cruise ship calls increased, so did criticism of their environmental impacts at sea and in port. Their diesel engines emitted soot into the atmosphere, not only when sailing but at the dock (since the engines produced the ships' electric power). To reduce water pollution, the Port, the state Department of Ecology, and the Northwest Cruise Ship Association signed a memorandum of understanding that banned discharge of untreated sewage, encouraged better wastewater management, and required monitoring of discharges. In 2005, Seattle became the second port in the nation where properly equipped cruise ships could plug into power from shore instead of running their engines, eliminating all air emissions. Seattle was the first city in the nation to provide two shore-power berths. In conjunction with Seattle City Light, the Port provided a new power connection at Terminal 30 for Princess Cruises and Holland America ships specially designed to use the new technology.

Seattle's cargo shipping also grew rapidly in the first half of the decade. Dramatic increases in container traffic were, ironically, aided by the first major work stoppage on West Coast docks since the 1971 longshore workers strike that closed Seattle and other ports for several months. In September 2002, a dispute over wages and new labor-saving technologies between the Pacific Maritime Association, representing shipping and stevedoring employers, and the International Longshore and Warehouse Union led to a lockout by the employers that closed all West Coast ports for 11 days. The subsequent cargo backups and shipping delays lasted for months after a federal judge ordered work to resume. Ultimately, because southern California ports faced a large backlog of ships waiting to unload and shortages of trucks and train cars to move containers, shippers diverted traffic to less-congested Seattle, Tacoma, Vancouver, and other Northwest ports.

The extra traffic helped boost Seattle (and Tacoma) container volume to record levels. Some shippers returned to California once the backlog cleared, but others, impressed by the Port of Seattle's proximity to rail lines and interstate highways, made the move permanent. Also contributing to Seattle's gains in container cargo were distribution centers that large importers like Home Depot, Target, Walmart Stores, and Pier 1 Imports set up in the Puget Sound area. In 2004 and again in 2005, the Port of Seattle saw the greatest growth in container traffic of any U.S. port, setting new records both years and in 2005 reaching its all-time high of more than two million import and export TEUs (20-foot equivalent units), for a total 14.5 million metric tons of containerized cargo. Volume remained high until the economic recession that began in 2008 brought sharp drops in container traffic worldwide. The Port's grain exports continued to increase even as container traffic leveled off. After Louis Dreyfus Commodities began operating Terminal 86 in March 2000, grain volume tripled in less than a decade as the company worked with the Port on significant improvements to the grain elevator. In 2008, 6.4 million metric tons of grain — mostly corn, soybeans, and sorghum from the Midwest — were shipped to China, Japan, and other Asian markets from the Terminal 86 grain elevator, setting an all-time record.

ABOVE: The Port had record-setting container traffic tonnage in 2004 and 2005, partly due to new relationships formed as a result of shippers diverting vessels to Seattle after a labor dispute in 2002.

OPPOSITE TOP: Sea-Tac's Central Terminal features a 60-foot-tall, 350-foot-wide window wall overlooking the airfield.

BELOW: A night view of Sea-Tac's Central Terminal from the airfield. The tower is used to control ground traffic, while a much taller tower nearby is operated by the FAA for air traffic control.

ENVIRONMENTAL RESTORATION

When progressive reformers conceived of public port districts at the start of the twentieth century and created the Port of Seattle in 1911, few if any foresaw that, long before the century's end, preventing and reversing environmental degradation would be among the most pressing issues facing the region and indeed the world. But the port district structure they created, combining the government powers of taxation, eminent domain, issuing bonds and more with an entrepreneurial, commercially driven business orientation, has proved particularly effective for dealing with some of the more intractable problems caused by a century of largely unfettered development and industrial pollution. Because of the size and scale of its operations, the Port felt the effects of the environmental movement early on, as it responded to activists' concerns and increasingly stringent state and federal regulations.

Long before current CEO Tay Yoshitani set the challenge for the Port of Seattle to be a national leader in sustainability, the Port was working to reduce air and water pollution in the harbor and at the airport, and to begin reversing the effects of prior pollution. The Port was able to do so for several reasons. Given the nature of its mission, it controlled and often altered large tracts of environmentally critical shorelines and wetlands, often in areas subject to significant degradation over the years. And its "public enterprise" structure allowed the Port to acquire and restore contaminated properties for environmentally sensitive future development that might be decades away, when neither other governmental bodies nor private companies were in a position to do so.

As one example, Terminal 117 on the Duwamish Waterway, formerly home to an asphalt manufacturing plant, is a federally designated Superfund site because of high levels of PCBs (polychlorinated biphenyls) and other contaminants. In 1999, the Port acquired the property and, with the City of Seattle, initiated a long-term joint project to clean up the site and the surrounding neighborhood. Over the next decade the Port removed contaminated soil, asphalt, oil, pipes, underground storage tanks, and debris from the site and offshore intertidal zone while working with the city, the community, and the federal Environmental Protection Agency (EPA) to prepare a comprehensive long-term clean-up plan for the area.

In 2001, when the EPA designated the entire Duwamish Waterway as a Superfund site,

the Port's substantial property holdings (including much of the waterway bed and more than 200 acres of uplands) gave it a central role in efforts to restore the environment while retaining critical water-dependent businesses along the river. Although a federally mandated cleanup was not scheduled to begin until 2012, in 2008 the Port, with input from the city, Washington State Department of Ecology, local businesses and community groups, began work on the Lower Duwamish River Habitat Conservation Plan. Adopted by the Port Commission in 2009, the plan identified 31 separate restoration project sites, comprising nearly 70 acres (approximately 30,000 lineal feet of shoreline) of new habitat. Even before then, the Port had (with an assist from the U.S. Army Corps of Engineers, Fish and Wildlife Service, and EPA) implemented considerable habitat enhancement efforts along the Duwamish aimed at promoting salmon recovery and improved refuge and feeding opportunities for wildlife.

To construct the third runway at Sea-Tac Airport, the Port needed to relocate a portion of Miller Creek near the airport, fill 13.46 acres of wetlands, and temporarily disturb another acre of wetland. To compensate, the Port restored and improved 102 acres of forested wetlands and provided fish habitat in the highly urbanized area next to the busy airport, in the midst of runway construction. The Port also selected a site on the Green River in Auburn to provide 65 acres of waterfowl habitat (which could not be created at or near the airport because of the hazard of aircraft striking birds). Mitigation work, mostly between 2004 and 2006, was followed by a planned 15-year monitoring program.

The Port also has been in the forefront of work to promote cleaner fuel and reduce air pollution and greenhouse gas emissions from trucks, ships, and machinery at the seaport, and to cut emissions and improve air quality at the airport. Since 1998, maintenance at the more than 60 acres of Port parks and public access sites has been 100 percent organic. Back in the 1970s, Sea-Tac was the nation's first airport to employ a full-time wildlife biologist to manage wildlife and habitat to minimize bird hazards, protecting both travelers and wildlife. Starting in 2007, the wildlife management staff teamed with University of Illinois researchers on a demonstration site for avian radar, making Sea-Tac the first airport in the country to use an advanced new tracking system with real-time displays of bird activity. Also at Sea-Tac, the Port designed and implemented an award-winning program that recycles nearly one quarter of the airport's total waste and introduced coordinated waste collection from arriving airplanes, promoting recycling while reducing emissions from multiple trash pickups.

ACCOUNTABILITY AND SUSTAINABILITY

Sea-Tac Airport opened its first major new terminal facility in 30 years on June 15, 2004. Along with the integrated baggage and security systems designed after 9/11 (and among the first such systems in the country), the new Concourse A and south terminal expansion added 14 gates and four baggage carousels. The new facility also displayed major public artworks and impressive architecture. The new Central Terminal, which opened in May 2005, featured a 60-foot-tall, 350-foot-long glass wall, which offered a panoramic view of takeoffs and landings. The central terminal also featured 20 new restaurants and shops for passengers, all operating under the Port's new "street pricing" policy, which limited prices at airport concessions to amounts charged by the same or comparable businesses outside the airport.

In 2004, the state Supreme Court rejected most of the legal challenges to the third runway, and on August 19 of that year the Airport Communities Coalition withdrew its remaining appeals, allowing construction to resume. Although the coalition failed to stop the project, its long-term opposition coincided with increased regulatory controls of environmental mitigation, including improved quality of fill dirt, state-of-the-art storm water treatment, relocation of a salmon-spawning stream, and creation or enhancement of wetlands. More than 13 million cubic yards of fill were delivered (another 3 million cubic yards came from on-site excavation) to build up a plateau held in place by three huge retaining walls (the largest is 1,430 feet long and 130 feet high, the tallest of its kind in North America). The 8,500-foot-long, 150-foot-wide, 17-inch-deep concrete runway constructed on this plateau opened on November 20, 2008.

Controversy over the runway did not end when the litigation did. In December 2007, a state auditor's report of the Port's capital program claimed the Port had wasted millions in construction contracts, mostly related to the third runway, and called its construction management "vulnerable to fraud, waste and abuse."

The Port responded by conducting its own investigations and implementing numerous financial reporting reforms. Later, the U.S. Justice Department, which had initiated its own investigation, closed it without pursuing any criminal indictments.

When Tay Yoshitani, a U.S. Army veteran who had worked at ports around the country and had headed the ports of Oakland and Baltimore, took the helm, he stressed ethics and transparency as central to the Port's mission, and the Port became one of the few in the country to establish a Workplace Responsibility Program, including an employee Code of Conduct.

ABOVE TOP: Taking the helm as CEO in 2007, Tay Yoshitani set a course for sustainability, challenging Port employees, tenants, and customers to implement cleaner operating strategies to make Seattle The Green Gateway.

ABOVE: Crews pour 130,000 cubic yards of concrete and 35,000 tons of asphalt to build Sea-Tac's 150-foot-wide, 17-inch-deep third runway.

OPPOSITE LEFT: The Terminal 5 redevelopment involved cleanup and restoration of contaminated industrial property.

RIGHT: Port employee Monica Bradley volunteers for an Earth Day cleanup along the Duwamish Waterway.

TOP: Kristi Hagen, a member of Local 98, became one of the first female "walking bosses," as ILWU foremen are called, on the Seattle waterfront, 1997.

BELOW: The automated arm at the Terminal 86 grain facility delivers grain to the hold of a ship. Terminal 86 has a capacity of four million bushels.

In addition to ethics, Yoshitani focused on environmental stewardship, which he saw as a competitive edge for Seattle, complementing the Port's mission to promote economic growth. Building on prior efforts, the Port continued working to restore habitat, reduce air and water pollution at the seaport and airport, clean up existing contaminants ranging from creosote-treated pilings to old fuel storage tanks, and conserve energy and reduce greenhouse gas emissions. With climate change a front-burner issue, the Port commissioned Herbert Engineering to analyze the carbon footprint of different trade routes between major Asian cities and central U.S. distribution centers. The 2009 study found that shipments to Puget Sound and then by rail to the Midwest produced significantly lower carbon emissions than shipments through other West Coast ports or via the Panama Canal. The Port promoted Puget Sound as The Green Gateway for maritime trade between Asia and a broad swath of the United States. Moreover, with significant and broad environmental programs instituted at Sea-Tac Airport, the title "Green Gateway" encompassed all Port operations. An independent report released in August 2007 stated that the combined environmental efforts at the airport made the Sea-Tac environmental program one of the strongest at any airport in the nation. A year later, Sea-Tac was named winner of the 2008 Environmental Achievement Award from Airports Council International – North America.

Promoting trade through Puget Sound was emblematic of the evolving relationships among area ports from occasionally bitter rivalries to regionalized and cooperative. The study of carbon emissions from Asian trade built on prior collaboration between the Seattle and Tacoma ports, including a 2006 inventory of air emissions from maritime sources on the Sound and subsequent efforts involving other ports, the transportation industry, regulatory agencies, and labor, environmental, and community groups, to set goals for reducing those emissions.

Port commissioners from Seattle and Tacoma collaborated on regional promotion and environmental concerns, as well as transportation infrastructure and port security issues. Seattle CEO Yoshitani emerged as a leader of the West Coast initiative to promote the U.S. West Coast as the optimal gateway for Asian cargo to and from the U.S. interior. He also worked with officials from other ports to lobby Congress for more funding for regional road and rail projects and environmental programs and to support President Barack Obama's 2010 call to double U.S. exports within 10 years.

TOP: Hong Kong-based Orient Overseas Container Line vessel enters port in 2004. OOCL is one of eight steamship lines calling at Terminal 18, operated by SSA Terminals.

BOTTOM: Longshore workers in orange safety vests are barely visible next to the huge post-Panamax cranes loading containers onto chassis beds. August 10, 2007.

ABOVE: Sea-Tac's largest airline customer, Alaska Airlines, makes its first landing on the new third runway in 2008.

RIGHT: Spiraling like a helix, Sea-Tac's eight-floor parking garage has electronic indicators on each level to help drivers locate available parking spaces.

LEFT: *Carnival Spirit*, a Carnival ship homeported in Seattle, moors at Terminal 91.

ABOVE: Enormous blue plugs provide shore power to cruise ships, so they do not need to run diesel engines to generate electricity while at berth. This helps eliminate harmful emissions from moored ships and helps preserve Seattle's air quality.

FACING THE NEXT CENTURY

Growing cooperation among regional ports was perhaps inevitable given the difficulties faced in the worldwide economic downturn that followed the collapse of the U.S. housing market. At the Port of Seattle, container traffic showed the impact of recession first, dropping sharply in 2008 and again in 2009. In contrast, the numbers of air and of cruise ship passengers both reached record highs in 2008, as did grain exports. With the recession deepening, 2009 saw declines in all those areas, but in the 2010 cruise season Seattle rebounded with new records for both passengers and ship calls. The Port responded aggressively to the economic downturn, cutting costs to keep operating in the black. Acknowledging the economic hard times, the commission cut its tax levy for 2010 and committed to using revenues, not taxes, to fund future capital programs at the seaport (consistent with the policy long in place at the airport).

Despite the downturn, 2009 brought some notable milestones for the Port. At the start of the cruise season, the Smith Cove Cruise Terminal, a new permanent two-berth cruise facility, opened at Pier 91, replacing the temporary cruise berths at Terminal 30. Like the temporary berths, the new Smith Cove terminal had land-based power connections, eliminating air pollution from ship engines. Later that summer, Terminal 30 returned to use as a container terminal and expanded (incorporating what had been

ABOVE TOP: With nearly 381,000 aircraft operations a year, Sea-Tac Airport accommodates 24 domestic and international airline companies.

BOTTOM: Sea-Tac's international arrivals hall welcomes travelers with a dramatic 70-foot-high wall of glass. The restored 1928 Alexander Eaglerock biplane and a replica of the high-tech Voyager aircraft (not visible in this photo) soar overhead. Both planes are on loan from the Museum of Flight.

Terminal 28), serving Matson Navigation and China Shipping in an agreement with SSA Terminals.

With the new third runway in use, the Port rebuilt Sea-Tac's oldest and longest runway, using 120,000 cubic yards of new and recycled concrete for the 11,901-foot-long, 20-inch-deep runway. Sound Transit's Central Link light rail, which had opened earlier in the year from Seattle to Tukwila, just short of the airport, finally arrived at the gate with the December 19, 2009, opening of the new City of SeaTac/Airport station. The Port worked closely with Sound Transit to accommodate the station and provide an attractive pedestrian bridge and walkway directly from the station to the terminal.

By 2010, the last year of its first century, the Port was well into planning for its second hundred years. Work began in 2008 on creating the "Century Agenda," a new 25-year strategic plan. As it looked to a new century, the Port in some respects had come full circle, while in others it was entering uncharted territory. Just as preparing for the 1914 opening of the Panama Canal helped drive creation of the Port of Seattle, the expected 2014 completion of a $5 billion project to build new larger locks on the canal figured prominently in the Port of Seattle's planning for the future. The enlarged canal would allow large container ships carrying cargo from Asia, now limited to West Coast ports, to reach Gulf and Atlantic ports, increasing competition and requiring even greater efforts on Seattle's part to retain its share of trade.

But while preparing for the anticipated reopening of a larger canal harks back to the Port's early days, it also illustrates that the climate in which the Port operates is very different from that when the Port was created. As noted, one way the Port has addressed potential competition from eastern ports is showing that trade through Puget Sound contributes less to global warming than do other routes, including through the canal. So a worldwide threat that was unknown when the canal and the Port were new may play a significant role in whether and how the newly widened canal affects trade through Seattle. Or, in time, the changing climate may make the canal less significant and open up a whole new set of challenges and opportunities. As the arctic ice cap shrinks, the until-now mythical Northwest Passage sought by explorers from the time the first Europeans ventured to the Pacific Northwest may become a reality, allowing cargo ships to cross the Arctic Ocean directly between Asia and Europe. How, if at all, that would affect the Port of Seattle is just one of many complexities the Port faces as it plans for the next quarter century and beyond.

As it does so, the Port stands on the firm foundation of all it has accomplished in its first 100 years. The success of its overriding mission — to use the public resources entrusted to it to promote trade and commerce, generate economic growth, and create jobs — is demonstrated by studies attesting to the Port's crucial economic impact on the region. Sea-Tac Airport, the marine terminals, Fishermen's Terminal, and other Port-owned facilities combine to directly generate almost 120,000 jobs; Sea-Tac alone produces nearly 90,000 jobs, the seaport another 22,000, commercial fishing 5,600, and the cruise industry more than 1,900. Spending by these workers, who earn $3.8 billion annually, creates more than $5 billion in regional economic activity, producing many thousands more jobs indirectly supported by Port activity. Businesses operating in Port facilities take in more than $17 billion in revenue and pay $876 million in local and state taxes, with airport businesses also paying $439 million in federal aviation taxes.

As significant as the statistics are, perhaps the most vivid illustration of what the Port has achieved comes from viewing Elliott Bay, the great natural harbor that was Seattle's reason for being from the time of its founding. Whether from a ferry or cruise ship arriving in the harbor or from a restaurant deck or public plaza at the Bell Street Pier, that view bears little resemblance to the dirty, confused tangle of wooden railroad trestles and small piers that prompted the push for a public port. And many of the most prominent landmarks along the entire sweep of waterfront — from the Smith Cove piers

ABOVE: Terminal 46, operated by Total Terminals International, with a towering city backdrop. In 2010, Terminal 46's post-Panamax cranes handled 188 container ships and served seven steamship lines.

FOLLOWING PAGES: Seattle's waterfront, 2010. Now shifted south of the central waterfront area, cargo operations and maritime industry coexist with tourism, recreation, and environmental restoration.

WATERFRONT ACCESS

From the start, along with constructing facilities for trade, commerce, and industry, the Port of Seattle has worked to develop parks and other sites for public access and recreation on the waterfront. Before the Port was created, there were no park areas along Seattle's central waterfront. In response, one of the Port's first projects was the creation of a "public waterfront observatory and playground" on the roof of its warehouse and headquarters building on the Bell Street Pier. The rooftop park opened in 1915 with assistance from the Seattle Park Board, which provided park benches, swings and sandboxes, and trees and flowers planted in tubs.

An early port publication touted the "inspiring glimpses of water traffic and the panorama of city and sea, forest and mountain" that tourists could catch from the park, and emphasized the advantages of the playground as a place for downtown shoppers to take their children:

> Conveniently, with practically no expense, at a place easily reached
> by Seattle mothers who patronize the big department stores and the
> fresh meat and vegetable markets, the Port Commission in "preparing
> for Panama," also provided a new "Happy-land" for the kiddies.

Unfortunately that first rooftop park lasted only a few years. It turned out that many park visitors were not tourists or shoppers' children but sailors and their dates from the streets (giving the innocent phrase "Happy-land" a whole new meaning), and the roof was soon closed as a "moral nuisance." However, in subsequent years the Port developed many other parks and access points all around Elliott Bay and beyond.

Today more than 60 acres of Port waterfront property are open to the public for a wide range of recreational uses, including parks, plazas, bicycle and foot trails and paths, fishing piers, picnic areas, benches and viewing areas, wildlife habitat, shoreline access, small boat marinas, boat launches, an exercise course, and more. To the north, Shilshole Bay Marina in Ballard near the mouth of the Ship Canal has offered moorage to recreational boaters since the 1960s; a fishing pier and more than a mile of public promenade also serve those without boats. South of downtown, a string of viewpoints, shoreline paths, and parks dots both sides of the Duwamish. Port of Seattle parks also ring Elliott Bay, from Smith Cove Park west of Terminal 91 in Magnolia to Jack Block Park (named in honor of the longshoreman who served for more than 25 years as a Port of Seattle commissioner) in West Seattle at Terminal 5. On the central waterfront, the current Bell Street Terminal features public plazas, including a new rooftop park with benches and viewing telescopes situated in nearly the same location as the Port's original park of almost a century ago.

ABOVE: The four-star Envirostar-certified Bell Harbor Marina is the city's only central waterfront marina. It offers moorage for 70 vessels and hosts an annual classic boat show.

BELOW: The panoramic view from Smith Cove Park spans the cruise ship terminal, downtown Seattle, Alki Point, and on a clear day, Mount Rainier.

in the north, past the Terminal 86 grain elevator and the Port-run waterfront park below it, the Port's Pier 69 headquarters, the restaurants and rooftop park of Bell Street Pier, and the conference center, hotel, and condominiums across the street, to the towering container cranes lining the waterfront south of downtown and both sides of the East Waterway — exist because of the Port. Add in the jetliners passing overhead on their way to Sea-Tac Airport 12 miles south and Fishermen's Terminal and Shilshole Bay Marina out of sight behind the Queen Anne and Magnolia hills, and the physical manifestation accurately reflects the Port's many tangible and intangible impacts on the region.

Smith Cove (foreground) and Bell Street Pier (background right) cruise terminals handled 223 dockings and 931,698 revenue passengers in 2010. The cruise industry also generated $425 million in business revenue, $18.9 million in state and local taxes, and more than 4,000 direct, induced, and indirect jobs.

PORT OF SEATTLE COMMISSIONERS
AND YEARS OF SERVICE

Hiram M. Chittenden	1911 – 1915	J. Knox Woodruff	1969 – 1973
Charles E. Remsberg	1911 – 1919	Fenton Radford	1969 – 1970
Robert Bridges	1911 – 1919	Paul S. Friedlander	1970 – 1983
Dr. Carl A. Ewald	1915 – 1919	Henry L. Kotkins	1970 – 1983
T. S. Lippy	1918 – 1921	Jack S. Block	1974 – 2001
W. S. Lincoln	1919 – 1932	Henry T. Simonson	1974 – 1985
Dr. W. T. Christensen	1919 – 1922	Jim Wright	1984 – 1989
George B. Lamping	1921 – 1933	Ivar Haglund	1984 – 1985
George F. Cotterill	1922 – 1934	Henry M. Aronson	1985 – 1989
Smith M. Wilson	1932 – 1942	Patricia Davis	1986 – 2009
Horace P. Chapman	1932 – 1947	Paige Miller	1988 – 2005
J. A. Earley	1934 – 1952	Gary Grant	1990 – 1999
E. H. Savage	1942 – 1958	Paul Schell	1990 – 1997
A. B. Terry	1947 – 1948	Clare Nordquist	1998 – 2003
Gordon Rowe	1949 – 1954	Bob Edwards	2000 – 2007
C. H. Carlander	1951 – 1962	Lawrence T. Molloy	2002 – 2005
M. J. Weber	1954 – 1960	Alec Fisken	2004 – 2007
Captain Thomas McManus	1958 – 1964	Lloyd Hara	2006 – 2009
John M. Haydon	1960 – 1969	John Creighton	2005 –
Gordon Newell	1960 – 1963	Bill Bryant	2008 –
Frank R. Kitchell	1961 – 1973	Gael Tarleton	2008 –
Miner H. Baker	1963 – 1969	Tom Albro	2010 –
Robert W. Norquist	1963 – 1969	Rob Holland	2010 –
Merle D. Adlum	1964 – 1983		

OPPOSITE: Seattle's Smith Tower was under construction when the first Port commissioners took office in 1911. Burns Lyman Smith, son of L. C. Smith for whom the building is named, dreamed it would be "the world's highest outside of New York, and the firm would have a cachet that would help elevate sales of Smith's new product, the typewriter." The building opened with fanfare in 1914.

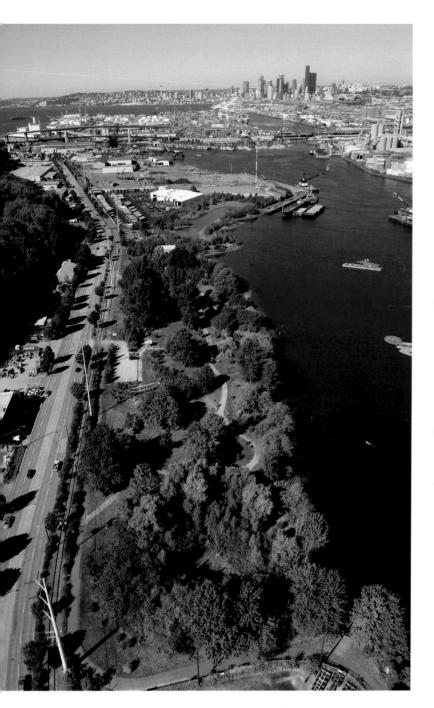

ABOVE: Terminal 107, a seven acre park with pathways, fish and wildlife habitat, and restored shoreline, is one of 20 public areas the Port maintains using organic landscaping.

RIGHT: Port of Seattle centennial lapel pin.

PORT OF SEATTLE GENERAL MANAGERS

From 1911 to 1933 there were no general managers per se of the Port of Seattle. Following the inception of the Port Commission, Hamilton Higday, assistant secretary of the commission, performed the duties of a general manager. Managers West, Bickford and Treadwell also held concurrent responsibilities as chief engineer. Later the position took the title of Executive Director, and in 2001 it was changed to Chief Executive Officer.

J. R. West	June 1933 – January 1935
Col. W. C. Bickford	January 1935 – November 1945
Col. Warren D. Lamport	February 1946 – September 1951
George T. Treadwell	October 1951 – July 1953
Howard M. Burke	November 1953 – June 1964
J. Eldon Opheim	July 1964 – January 1977
Richard D. Ford	January 1977 – June 1985
James D. Dwyer	July 1985 – September 1988
Zeger van Asch van Wijck	January 1989 – July 1992
Mic R. Dinsmore	August 1992 – March 2007
Tay Yoshitani	March 2007 – Present

PORT OF SEATTLE INTERNATIONAL LABOR PARTNERS AND AFFILIATED LOCAL UNIONS, 2011

Bricklayers and Allied Craft Workers (BAC)
>   Local 1

International Association of Heat and Frost Insulators and Allied Workers
>   Local 7

International Brotherhood of Boilermakers, Iron Ship Builders, Blacksmiths, Forgers, and Helpers
>   Local 502

International Brotherhood of Electrical Workers (IBEW)
>   Local 46

International Brotherhood of Teamsters (IBT)
>   Local 117
>   Local 174
>   Local 763

International Longshore and Warehouse Union (ILWU)
>   Local 9
>   Local 19
>   Local 32

International Union of Elevator Constructors (IUEC)
>   Local 19

International Union of Operating Engineers (IUOE)
>   Local 286
>   Local 302
>   Local 612

International Association of Machinists and Aerospace Workers (IAM)
>   Local 289

International Association of Fire Fighters (IAFF)
>   Local 1257

International Association of Bridge, Structural and Ornamental Iron Workers
>   Local 86

International Union of Painters and Allied Trades (IUPAT), District Council 5
>   Local 300
>   Local 1094

Laborers' International Union of North America (LIUNA)
>   Local 242
>   Local 440

Operative Plasterers and Cement Masons International Association (OP&CMIA)
>   Local 77
>   Local 528

United Association of Journeymen and Apprentices of the Plumbing and Pipefitting Industry
>   Local 32
>   Local 699

United Brotherhood of Carpenters and Joiners of America
>   Local 131

United Union of Roofers, Waterproofers and Allied Workers
>   Local 54

Sheet Metal Workers International Association
>   Local 66

Seattle/King County Building and Construction Trades Council

M.L. King County Labor Council

Washington State Labor Council

Union subcontractors, members of Roofers and Waterproofers Union Local 54, take a break from their work on the Consolidated Rental Car Facility at Sea-Tac.

A NOTE ON SOURCES

All works of history rest on a foundation of earlier work and this book is no exception. We drew heavily on the two prior published histories of the Port of Seattle: *A History of the Port of Seattle* by Padraic Burke, which appeared in 1975, and *Pioneers and Partnerships: A History of the Port of Seattle*, an adaptation and updating of Burke's work by Dick Paetzke, published two decades later. Equally valuable for its comprehensive and detailed account of the Port's formation and early years was the unpublished manuscript of a draft history of the Port prepared around 1970 by Bainbridge Island journalist Walt Woodward.

We relied on the work of many historians of Seattle and the Northwest for additional details of Port history as well as the broader historical context in which the Port developed. The following were particularly helpful: Richard Berner, *Seattle in the 20th Century*; Archie Binns, *Northwest Gateway: The Story of the Port of Seattle*; Paul Dorpat, *Seattle Waterfront: An Illustrated History*; Paul Dorpat and Genevieve McCoy, *Building Washington: A History of Washington State Public Works*; Robert E. Ficken, *Washington Territory* and *Washington State: The Inaugural Decade, 1889-1899*; Nard Jones, *Seattle*; Murray Morgan, *Skid Road: An Informal Portrait of Seattle*; Roger Sale, *Seattle Past To Present*; Sam L. Sutherland, "Fishermen's Terminal: Million-Dollar Industry," in *Magnolia: Making More Memories*; and Anne B. Swensson, *A Brief History of Seattle's South-Central Waterfront*.

Several publications prepared over the years by Port employees provided background on various aspects of Port history. These include *Port of Seattle: A Municipal Corporation Whose Stockholders are the Whole People of King County*, from 1915; *The Port of Seattle: A Case History in Public Port Development*, written in 1952 by George T. Treadwell, longtime Port chief engineer and general manager; and *Port in a Storm: An Historical Review of the Founding of the Port of Seattle*, published in 1971 on the Port's 70th anniversary. We also made significant use of primary and secondary source documents available on the Port's website (www.portseattle.org).

Finally, we turned repeatedly to work by our colleagues on HistoryLink.org, the Free Online Encyclopedia of Washington State History, among which must be singled out the comprehensive suite of essays on the history of Seattle-Tacoma International Airport by the greatly missed Walt Crowley, cofounder and first executive director of HistoryLink. Please go to HistoryLink.org for further information and sources on the Port of Seattle, public ports in Washington, and many of the historical figures and events discussed in this book.

ACKNOWLEDGMENTS

The authors wish to express their gratitude to the following kind folks for their invaluable assistance with the production of this book: Dusti Banazzio, Nancy Blanton, Jane Kilburn, Katie Nowlin, and Rob Walgren at the Port of Seattle; Thomas R. Speer, with Duwamish Tribal Services; Nancy Kinnear; and Marie McCaffrey, Tom Brown, and Charles Smyth, our colleagues at HistoryLink.org. We also wish to offer a nod to fellow writers who blazed earlier trails exploring various aspects of the Port of Seattle's history, among them: Archie Binns, Nard Jones, Roger Sale, Walt Woodward, Padraic Burke, Dick Paetzke, Paul Dorpat, and Walt Crowley. Finally, and especially, grateful thanks to Colleen O'Connor from Kit Oldham and to Kate Race from Peter Blecha for your support during this year-long project and always.

IMAGE CREDITS

FRONT COVER

View of waterfront, May 24, 1915. Courtesy Washington State Archives, Puget Sound Branch, Port of Seattle Photograph Collection.

FRONT COVER FLAP

Sea-Tac Airport, Opening Day, 1949. Courtesy Washington State Archives, Puget Sound Branch, Port of Seattle Photograph Collection.

FRONT END PAPERS

Bird's Eye View: Seattle and Environs. Augustus Koch, 1891. Courtesy University of Washington Libraries, Special Collections, (MAP 123).

TITLE PAGE

Seattle's Waterfront, 1874. By Asahel Curtis. Courtesy Washington State Archives, Puget Sound Branch (AR-28001001-ph002117).

COPYRIGHT

The World Port of Seattle and Its Ocean Trade Routes, Glenn Sheckels. Port of Seattle Annual Report, 1934. Port of Seattle Archives.

P. 4

Richard D. Ford at Terminal 37, 1983. Port of Seattle photo by Don Wilson.

P. 6 AND 7

Aerial View of Seattle, 1878. Courtesy University of Washington Libraries, Special Collections (MAP 119).

P. 8

Coal Bunkers. Lawrence Denny Lindsey. Courtesy Museum of History and Industry, 2002.3.1643.

P. 10

Logs await shipment at King Street Coal Bunkers, Seattle, Washington, 1889. Courtesy University of Washington Libraries, Special Collections (BAB 43).

Post card: Seattle waterfront, ca. 1907. Port of Seattle Archives.

Post card: Delivery wagons of the Seattle Coal and Fuel Co., Railroad Ave. S. and Dearborn St., ca. 1909. Courtesy University of Washington Libraries, Special Collections (SEA 1789).

Post card: Railroad Avenue looking north. Courtesy University of Washington Libraries, Special Collections (UW 27022z).

P. 11

King Street Coal Docks. Courtesy Washington State Archives.

P. 12 AND 13

Yesler's Wharf. Courtesy Washington State Archives, Puget Sound Branch, Port of Seattle Photograph Collection.

Eastern Washington logging. Courtesy Washington State Archives, Puget Sound Branch, Port of Seattle Photograph Collection.

Lumber mill, early 1900s. Courtesy Washington State Archives, Puget Sound Branch, Port of Seattle Photograph Collection.

Duwamish and Seattle Harbor, 1854. Courtesy Peter Blecha Archives.

P. 14

Burning of Seattle from the Docks, 1891. Courtesy Washington State Archives.

Columbia and Puget Sound Railway Station and Docks, ca. 1882. Courtesy University of Washington Libraries, Special Collections, (A. Curtis 26436, UW 5852).

P. 15

James J. Hill. Courtesy National Archives.

Thomas Burke. Courtesy Museum of History and Industry, (SHS 12455).

P. 16

Passengers on Victoria, *ca. 1904-1910.* Courtesy Puget Sound Maritime Historical Society (2635-945 and 2635-947).

Alaska Steamship Company brochure. Courtesy Bjorn Larsson, Timetable Images.

P. 17

Puget Sound's Mosquito Fleet. Courtesy Washington State Archives, Puget Sound Branch, Port of Seattle Photograph Collection.

P. 18 AND 19

Seattle waterfront, looking north. Courtesy University of Washington Libraries, Special Collections (SEA 0649).

P. 20

Railroad Avenue looking north. Courtesy Puget Sound Maritime Historical Society (1741-86).

P. 21

Reginald H. Thomson. Courtesy Seattle Municipal Archives (64766).

George F. Cotterill. Courtesy Seattle Municipal Archives (12280).

Robert Bridges. Port of Seattle Archives.

P. 22

Hiram M. Chittenden. Courtesy University of Washington Libraries, Special Collections (UW POR0022).

Opening of the Panama Canal, 1914. Courtesy Jimmy Carter Library.

Opening of the Hiram M. Chittenden Locks, 1917. Courtesy Washington State Archives, Puget Sound Branch, Port of Seattle Photograph Collection.

P. 23

George F. Cotterill. Courtesy University of Washington Libraries, Special Collections (UW 25806).

P. 24

Railroad Avenue, 1911. Courtesy Museum of History and Industry, PEMCO Webster and Stevens Collection (1983.10.6713).

P. 25

Pike Place Market, ca. 1907. Courtesy Washington State Archives.

P. 26

Loading of Acme Steel in hold of ship, ca. 1920s. Courtesy Washington State Archives, Puget Sound Branch, Port of Seattle Photograph Collection.

P. 28

Workers stack bales of Indian hemp, ca. 1926. Courtesy Washington State Archives, Puget Sound Branch, Port of Seattle Photograph Collection.

Post card: Harbor Island in 1912. Port of Seattle Archives.

Post card: The new plans for the development of Harbor Island. Courtesy University of Washington Libraries, Special Collections (UW 5987).

P. 29

Opening of Bell Street Pier Rooftop Park, 1915. Courtesy Washington State Archives, Puget Sound Branch, Port of Seattle Photograph Collection.

Bell Street Pier, 1915. Courtesy Washington State Archives, Puget Sound Branch, Port of Seattle Photograph Collection.

P. 30

Seattle, looking west from 1st Avenue and Yesler Way, ca. 1913. Courtesy University of Washington Libraries, Special Collections (UW 9939).

P. 31

Post card: The Great Northern Docks at Smith Cove and the Steamship Minnesota. Courtesy University of Washington Libraries, Special Collections (SEA 2159).

Fishermen's Terminal dedication, January 10, 1914. Courtesy Museum of History and Industry (SHS 15004).

The Port's ferry, Leschi, *operated on Lake Washington.* Port of Seattle Archives.

P. 32 AND 33

"Untitled (Panoramic of Smith Cove)," ca. 1880s, by Emily Inez Denny. Courtesy Museum of History and Industry (a1955.878.3).

Longshoremen loading Taiyu Maru *at Smith Cove, ca. 1916.* Courtesy Washington State Archives, Puget Sound Branch, Port of Seattle Photograph Collection.

Men unload silk. Courtesy Washington State Archives, Puget Sound Branch, Port of Seattle Photograph Collection.

Workers on tractors, Smith Cove, ca. 1916. Courtesy Washington State Archives, Puget Sound Branch, Port of Seattle Photograph Collection.

Workers load lumber with a locomotive crane at Smith Cove, ca. 1916. Courtesy Washington State Archives, Puget Sound Branch, Port of Seattle Photograph Collection.

Terminal 91, 2010. Port of Seattle photo by Don Wilson.

P. 34

Men load lumber with gantry crane at Smith Cove, ca. 1916. Courtesy Washington State Archives, Puget Sound Branch, Port of Seattle Photograph Collection.

P. 35

Loading Samson Brand Apples, Asahel Curtis. Courtesy Washington State Historical Society.

Schooners load grain at Hanford Street Grain Terminal. Courtesy Washington State Archives, Puget Sound Branch, Port of Seattle Photograph Collection.

P. 36

Robert Bridges and Family. Courtesy Bridges Family.

P. 37

Launching of the ship Snoqualmie, *August 1919.* Courtesy Museum of History and Industry (SHS 3533).

P. 38 AND 39

Men load silk. Courtesy Museum of History and Industry (SHS 1221).

Silk train and steamships Minnesota *and* Dakota *at Smith Cove.* Port of Seattle Archives.

Panorama of Seattle waterfront, 1917. Courtesy Library of Congress.

Advertisement, Port of Seattle Annual Report, 1928. Port of Seattle Archives.

P. 40

Fishermen spear their catch, ca. 1920s. Courtesy Washington State Archives, Puget Sound Branch, Port of Seattle Photograph Collection.

P. 42

Lumber in 1937. Courtesy Washington State Archives, Puget Sound Branch, Port of Seattle Photograph Collection.

Labeling canned salmon. Courtesy Washington State Archives, Puget Sound Branch, Port of Seattle Photograph Collection.

P. 43

Hooverville, 1941. Courtesy Washington State Archives, Puget Sound Branch, Port of Seattle Photograph Collection.

Hooverville, 1930s. Port of Seattle Archives.

Hooverville, 1941. Courtesy Washington State Archives, Puget Sound Branch, Port of Seattle Photograph Collection.

Hooverville mail sign. Courtesy Museum of History and Industry (1980.7029.1).

P. 44

Port of Seattle Annual Report cover, 1933. Port of Seattle Archives.

Washington State apples, in storage at Port warehouse, ca. 1920s. Courtesy Washington State Archives.

P. 45

Matt H. Gormley Port auditor, during his days in the Second Infantry. Courtesy Washington State Archives.

Railroad Avenue, 1934. Courtesy Seattle Municipal Archives (8991).

P. 46

Policemen post behind bales of hay. Courtesy Museum of History and Industry, *Seattle Post-Intelligencer* Collection (PI 24007).

P. 47

Strikers block a train during the Battle of Smith Cove, 1934. Courtesy Museum of History and Industry, *Seattle Post-Intelligencer* Collection (PI 24001).

P. 48 AND 49

Longshoremen painstakingly load break bulk cargo. Courtesy Washington State Archives, Puget Sound Branch, Port of Seattle Photograph Collection.

ILWU member loads Washington State apples, Terminal 91. Port of Seattle photo by Don Wilson.

ILWU hiring hall, 1981. Port of Seattle photo by Don Wilson.

Moving cargo with forklift. Courtesy Washington State Archives, Puget Sound Branch, Port of Seattle Photograph Collection.

P. 50

Strikers at the entrance of Smith Cove, 1934. Courtesy Museum of History and Industry, *Seattle Post-Intelligencer* Collection (PI 24004).

P. 51

Sailors at Bell Street Pier, ca. 1930s. Courtesy Washington State Archives, Puget Sound Branch, Port of Seattle Photograph Collection.

Hanford Street Grain Terminal, ca. 1940. Courtesy Washington State Archives, Puget Sound Branch, Port of Seattle Photograph Collection.

P. 52

Seattle Army Port of Embarkation. Courtesy Coast Guard Museum.

Sailors ship out at the Port of Embarkation. Courtesy Museum of History and Industry (1986.5.10558.1).

P. 53

Airport ground breaking, January 2, 1943. Port of Seattle Archives.

The first landing at Sea-Tac, October 31, 1944. Courtesy Washington State Archives, Puget Sound Branch, Port of Seattle Photograph Collection.

P. 54

Sea-Tac Airport, 1950s. Courtesy Washington State Archives, Puget Sound Branch, Port of Seattle Photograph Collection.

P. 56

Smith Cove docks. Courtesy Washington State Archives, Puget Sound Branch, Port of Seattle Photograph Collection.

1944 Port of Seattle "Victory Book" cover. Port of Seattle Archives.

P. 57

Strikers, 1947. Courtesy Museum of History and Industry, *Seattle Post-Intelligencer* Collection (PI 24163).

P. 58 AND 59

Salmon Bay Post Card. Courtesy University of Washington Libraries, Special Collections (SEA 1924).

Fishermen's Terminal 1936. Courtesy Seattle Municipal Archives (10525).

Fishermen's Terminal, 1913. Courtesy Washington State Archives, Puget Sound Branch, Port of Seattle Photograph Collection.

Fishermen's Terminal, 2004. Port of Seattle photo by Don Wilson.

Foreign Trade Zone No. 5. Port of Seattle Archives.

P. 60

Sea-Tac Airport control tower, 1944. Courtesy Washington State Archives, Puget Sound Branch, Port of Seattle Photograph Collection.

Architect's drawing. Port of Seattle Archives.

P. 61

Ethiopian Emperor Haile Selassie at Sea-Tac, 1954. Port of Seattle Archives.

Sea-Tac Post Card. Port of Seattle Archives.

P. 62 AND 63

Main terminal, July 9, 1949. Courtesy Washington State Archives, Puget Sound Branch, Port of Seattle Photograph Collection.

Sea-Tac lounge, 1950. Port of Seattle Archives.

P. 64 AND 65

The first airport terminal, 1947. Courtesy Washington State Archives, Puget Sound Branch, Port of Seattle Photograph Collection, Ray Bishop Scrapbook.

Dedication of the new terminal; 30,000 visitors; Northwest Airlines Crew July 9, 1949. Courtesy Washington State Archives, Puget Sound Branch, Port of Seattle Photograph Collection.

Sea-Tac aerial with four cross-wind runways. Courtesy Washington State Archives, Puget Sound Branch, Port of Seattle Photograph Collection.

Northwest Airlines at Sea-Tac, 1949. Courtesy Washington State Archives, Puget Sound Branch, Port of Seattle Photograph Collection.

Post card: Sea-Tac Administration Building, 1949. Port of Seattle Archives.

P. 66

Land survey at Shilshole, 1957. Port of Seattle Archives.

Shilshole Bay Marina, 1963. Port of Seattle Archives.

P. 67

Longshoremen loading cargo, 1950s. Port of Seattle Archives.

1957 Port of Seattle Annual Report Cover. Port of Seattle Archives.

P. 68

Miss Maritime of 1961, Julie Blonk. Port of Seattle Archives.

P. 70

Harry Bridges. Courtesy Museum of History and Industry, *Seattle Post-Intelligencer* Collection (1986.5.19895).

Cargo booms and containers on ship. Port of Seattle Archives.

P. 71

Loading Alaska Steamship containers. Port of Seattle Archives.

P. 72

Break bulk cargo; Loading Cases of Salmon; Loading Trailers. Courtesy Washington State Archives, Puget Sound Branch, Port of Seattle Photograph Collection.

Container crane and ship. Port of Seattle Archives.

P. 73

Vintage Shilshole Bay Marina sign, 1963. Port of Seattle Archives.

P. 74

Sea-Tac construction, 1970. Port of Seattle Archives.

Tyree Scott leads protest at Sea-Tac, 1969. Port of Seattle Archives.

P. 75

Post card: Fisher Flouring Mills on Harbor Island, 1914. Port of Seattle Archives.

Five ships dock at Pier 20. Port of Seattle Archives.

Aerial of Terminal 18 and East Waterway, 1967. Port of Seattle Archives.

P. 76

President John F. Kennedy and Air Force One at Sea-Tac, September 27, 1963. Port of Seattle Archives.

Robert F. Kennedy at Sea-Tac, March 26, 1968. Port of Seattle Archives.

President John F. Kennedy with Senator Magnuson at Sea-Tac. Courtesy *The Seattle Times.*

P. 77

Lyndon B. Johnson at Sea-Tac Airport, 1966. Courtesy Seattle Municipal Archives (63797).

P. 78

Seattle, looking north along the East Waterway, ca. 1965. Courtesy University of Washington Libraries, Special Collections (SEA 1626).

P. 79

Whirly crane Terminal 46, 1973. Port of Seattle Archives.

Public fishing pier at Pier 57 in 1968. Port of Seattle Archives.

P. 80

Terminal 25. Port of Seattle Archives.

P. 81

Liu Lin Hai *at Terminal 86.* Port of Seattle Archives.

Import cars at Terminal 91. Port of Seattle Archives.

P. 82

The crew of the Liu Lin Hai. Port of Seattle photo by Clyde Keller.

Liu Lin Hai *celebration.* Port of Seattle photo by Clyde Keller.

P. 83

China Air Cargo, 1980. Port of Seattle Archives.

Sea-Tac 25th anniversary special edition insert. Port of Seattle Archives.

P. 84

Waterfront in disrepair, 1986. Port of Seattle photo by Don Wilson.

P. 86

Pier 66 construction. Port of Seattle photo by Don Wilson.

P. 87

Flying Tiger Air Cargo, 1970s; Loading logs at Sea-Tac, 1985. Port of Seattle Archives.

Northwest cherries via China Airlines Cargo; Alaska Air Cargo. Port of Seattle photos by Don Wilson.

P. 88

Cappy Thompson, "I Was Dreaming of Spirit Animals." Port of Seattle Photo by Don Wilson.

Twin Stack rails cars 1985. Port of Seattle photo by Don Wilson.

P. 89

Ivar Haglund, 1983. Port of Seattle photo by Don Wilson.

Loading pulses of wheat seed, 1984. Port of Seattle photo by Don Wilson.

P. 90

Terminal 46, 1983. Port of Seattle photo by Don Wilson.

P. 91

Parking garage at Sea-Tac, 1992. Port of Seattle photo by Don Wilson.

Satellite Transit System, 1982. Port of Seattle Archives.

1985 Port of Seattle Annual Report. Port of Seattle Archives.

P. 92

Public Fishing Pier at Terminal 86, 1981. Port of Seattle Archives.

ILWU load apples at Terminal 91, 1986. Port of Seattle photo by Don Wilson.

P. 93

Seattle and NYK 100th anniversary commemorative booklet. Port of Seattle Archives.

Vessel Asian Venture *at Port terminal, 1991.* Port of Seattle photo by Don Wilson.

P. 94

Bell Street Pier and Cruise Terminal. Port of Seattle photo by Don Wilson.

P. 95

C.E.O. Mic Dinsmore at Pier 66. Port of Seattle photo by Don Wilson.

P. 96

Sea-Tac's Central Terminal. Port of Seattle photo by Don Wilson.

P. 98

Norwegian Star *at Bell Street Pier.* Port of Seattle photo by Don Wilson.

P. 99

President Bill Clinton presents during WTO. Port of Seattle photo by Dan Lamont.

P. 100

Interior of Central Terminal at Sea-Tac. Port of Seattle photo by Don Wilson.

Exterior of Central Terminal at Sea-Tac. Port of Seattle photo by Don Wilson.

P. 101

Hanjin at Terminal 46. Port of Seattle photo by Don Wilson.

P. 102

Clean up at Terminal 5. Port of Seattle Archives.

Port employee, Monica Bradley, volunteers to restore the shoreline. Port of Seattle photo by Don Wilson.

P. 103

C.E.O. Tay Yoshitani. Port of Seattle photo by David Johanson Vasquez.

Third runway construction, 2007. Port of Seattle photo by Don Wilson.

P. 104

Kristi Hagen, Local 98, ILWU walking boss. Port of Seattle photo by Don Wilson.

Automated arm, Terminal 86 Grain Terminal. Port of Seattle photo by Don Wilson.

P. 105

Orient Overseas Container Line (OOCL) vessel, 2004. Port of Seattle photo by Don Wilson.

Cranes stack containers. Port of Seattle photo by Don Wilson.

P. 106

Alaska Airlines makes its first landing on the new, third runway. Port of Seattle photo by Don Wilson.

Sea-Tac parking garage at night. Port of Seattle photo by Don Wilson.

P. 107

Carnival Spirit *at Terminal 91.* Port of Seattle photo by Don Wilson.

Cruise ship shore power. Port of Seattle photo by Don Wilson.

INDEX

P. 108

International carriers. Port of Seattle photo by Don Wilson.

Gina Marie Lindsey Arrivals Hall, Sea-Tac. Port of Seattle photo by Don Wilson.

P. 109

Terminal 46 and Seattle skyline at night. Port of Seattle photo by Don Wilson.

P. 110 AND 111

Elliott Bay, Downtown Seattle and Skyline, Terminals 18, 30 and 46. Port of Seattle photo by Don Wilson.

P. 112

Bell Harbor Marina. Port of Seattle photo by Don Wilson.

Smith Cove Park. Port of Seattle photo by Don Wilson.

P. 113

Terminals 91, 86, Elliott Bay and downtown Seattle looking south. Port of Seattle photo by Don Wilson.

P. 114

Smith Tower and Waterfront, 1914. Port of Seattle Archives.

P. 116

Terminal 107 Park and Duwamish Waterway, looking north. Port of Seattle photo by Don Wilson.

P. 117

Roofers at Consolidated Rental Car Facility. Port of Seattle photo by Don Wilson.

BACK END PAPERS

Seattle and Environs, 2010. Port of Seattle photo by Don Wilson.

BACK COVER FLAP

Author photos: Kit Oldham. Courtesy Steve Schneider. *Peter Blecha.* Courtesy Ken Myer.

BACK COVER

Gina Marie Lindsey Arrivals Hall, Seattle-Tacoma International Airport, 2011. Port of Seattle photo by Don Wilson.

Terminal 46 and Seattle skyline, 2005. Port of Seattle photo by Don Wilson.

1964 Civil Rights Act, 76

9/11, 98-100

A

Adlum, Merle, 79, 115

Airport Communities Coalition, 91, 97, 103

Alaska Air Cargo, 87

Alaska Airlines, 106

Alaska Steamship Company, 16, 71

Alaskan Way, 9, 44, 94–95, 97

Alki, 12

American Hawaiian Steamship Company, 61

American Mail Line, 69

American President Lines, 80, 88

American Shipowners Association, 57

Ames Terminal, 66,

APEC (Asia-Pacific Economic Cooperation), 99

APL (American President Lines), 80, 88, 90

Army Port of Embarkation (piers 36, 37, 38, 39), 52

Asian Venture, 92

Asia-Pacific Economic Cooperation (APEC) conference, 99

Associated Shipyards, 75

Ayers, R. F., 28-30

B

Ballard, 22, 58, 66, 112

Battle of Smith Cove, 32, 46, 50, 57

Beck, Dave, 46

Bell Harbor Marina, 95, 97, 112

Bell Street Pier, 29, 31, 51, 52, 86, 94-95, 98, 109, 112, 113

Bell Street Pier Cruise Terminal, 98

Bell Street Terminal, 17, 34, 98, 112

Bellingham, 17

Bigler, Earle S., 64

Black Tuesday, 41–42

Blake Island State Park, 99

Block, Jack, 82, 112, 115

Blonk, Julie, 69

Boeing Airplane Company, 53, 55. *See also* Boeing Company, The

Boeing Bust, 76–77

Boeing Company, The, 53, 60, 76–77, 86, 87, 99

Boeing Field, 53, 60, 64

Boeing Plant 1, 77

Boeing Spares Distribution Center, 87

Boeing, Bill, 87

Bogue, Virgil G., 16, 20–21, 28

Booz, Allen & Hamilton, 67, 69

Bow Lake, 52, 53, 60

Bradley, Monica, 103

Bridges, Harry, 46, 49, 57, 71

Bridges, Robert, 20, 21, 24–25, 29, 34–35, 36, 37–38, 49, 115

Burien, 91

Burke, Howard M., 61, 66, 116

Burke, Padraic, 36, 46, 56, 67, 77, 118, 119

Burke, Thomas, 14–16, 20

Burke-Gilman Trail, 14, 15

Bush Terminal Company, 28

Butler, Charles, 75

C

Calhoun, Scott, 24-25, 28

Canada-United States Free Trade Agreement, 92

Cargolux, 87

Carlander, Clarence H. , 61, 115

Carnival Spirit, 107

Carr, Edmund, 58

Central Contractors Association, 74

Central Waterfront Project, 94, 95

Century 21 Exposition, 66, 73

Chapman, Horace, 52, 53, 115

China Airlines Cargo, 83, 87

China Ocean Shipping Company (COSCO), 89

Chittenden, Hiram M., 22, 24, 28–29, 34, 37–38, 58, 115

City of Seattle, 28, 50, 93, 99,102

Civil Aeronautics Administration (CAA), 53, 64

Clinton, Bill, 99

Condit, Phil, 99

Cotterill, George F., 20, 21–22, 23, 24, 37, 42, 45, 115

Crowley, Walt, 36, 118, 119

D

Daffron, Shelvy, 50

Dakota, 16

Davis, Patricia "Pat," 94, 99, 115

Denny Hotel, 18

Denny party, 11, 12

Denny, Arthur T., 12

Denny, Emily Inez, 32

Denny, Mary, 12

Des Moines, 91

Dinsmore, Mic, 95, 116

Duwamish River, 13, 17, 21, 24, 28, 36, 43, 75, 112

Duwamish tribe, 12, 32, 75

Duwamish Waterway, 24, 36, 66, 73, 75, 77, 79, 80, 93–94, 102, 103

E

Earley, J. A., 45, 115

East Waterway Dock, 52, 59, 75

East Waterway, 27, 29–30, 31, 34, 35, 59, 75, 79, 113

Eastern Washington, 20, 34, 51, 59

Elliott Bay, 6, 9, 11, 12, 15, 20, 22, 32, 43, 75, 79, 100, 109, 112

Environmental Protection Agency (EPA), 75, 102

EVA Air Cargo, 87

Exact, 12

F

FAA (Federal Aviation Administration), 79, 91, 97, 101

Fairy, 17

Fay, Robert C., 12

Federal Aviation Administration (FAA), 79, 91, 97, 101

Federal Way, 91

FedEx Express Freight, 87

Foreign Trade Zones, 59, 92

Fisher Flouring Mills, 75

Fishermen's Terminal, 6, 27, 31, 58, 59, 108, 113

Flying Tiger Air Cargo, 87

Flying Tiger Line, 87

Foisie, Frank, 38

Ford, Richard D., 4, 5, 73, 116

Foreign Trade Zone No. 5, 59

Foreign Trade Zone Board, 92

Fortune, 93

Front Street, 9, 11

G

Gates, Bill, 99

Gilman, Daniel, 14

Gormley, Matt, 44, 45–46

Government Locks, 22

Great Depression, 7, 38, 39, 42–44, 51, 53, 56, 61, 77

Great Fire of 1889, 12, 15, 43

Great Northern Railway, 10, 15–16, 21, 28, 30, 32, 38, 50

Great Seattle Fire. *See* Great Fire of 1889

Griffiths & Sprague Stevedoring Company, 57

H

Hagen, Kristi, 104

Haglund, Ivar, 88, 89

Hanford Street Grain Terminal, 35, 51, 75

Hanjin Shipping Co., Ltd., 89

Harbor Island Terminal, 30

Harbor Island, 27–30, 43, 51, 52, 56, 59, 73, 75, 92

Harbor Lines Commission, 20

Hay, Marion E., 24

Herbert Engineering, 104

Highline School District, 91

Hill, James J., 15–16, 21

Holland America Line, 32, 100

Hoover, Herbert, 43

Hooverville, 42, 43, 51

Horizon Airlines, 90

Horton, Byron and Helen, 58

Hubbard, Eddie, 87

I

ILA Local 38-12, 35, 38, 46, 48–49

Interbay, 27, 32, 43

International Brotherhood of Teamsters, 117

International Longshore and Warehouse Union (ILWU), 48, 101, 117

International Longshoremen's Association (ILA), 46, 48, 50. *See also* ILA Local 38-12

International Teamsters Union, 46

Interstate Commerce Commission, 60

J

Jackson, Henry, 82

Jackson, Jesse, 43

Japan Six-Line, 81

K

Kennedy, John F., 69, 77

Kennedy, Joseph P., 51

Kennedy, Robert, 77

King County Board of Tideland Appraisers, 20

King County Economic Development Council, 77

King, Terry, 48

KING-TV, 67

KJR, 75

Klondike Gold Rush, 16, 22

Knights of Labor, 48

KOMO radio, 75

Korean Air Cargo, 87

Kotkins, Henry, 82, 115

L

Lake Washington Ship Canal, 22, 24, 112

Lamping, George B., 23, 37, 115

Lamport, Warren, 61, 116

Langlie, Arthur, 52, 64

Leonesa, 12

Leschi, 31, 34

Lin Zuyi, 89

Lincoln, W. S., 37–38, 115

Lindberg, William J., 76

Liu Lin Hai, 81, 82, 89

Locke, Gary, 99

Long-Bell Lumber Company, 42

Louis Dreyfus Commodities, 101

M

Magnolia, 27, 32, 94, 112, 113

Magnuson, Warren G., 52, 77, 82

Martinair Cargo, 87

Marvin, Fred, 52,

Matson Navigation Company, 89–90, 108

McChord Field, 53

McLean Trucking Co., 71

McLean, Malcolm, 71

McManus, Thomas, 67, 115

Mead, Albert E., 22

Mercer, Thomas, 12

Miller, Paige, 94, 115

Minnesota, 16, 31

Moldenhour, Herman A., 64

Moran, Robert, 43,

Mosquito Fleet, 10, 12, 13, 14, 17, 22, 27

Moxlie, Bob, 17

Muller, Clifford C., 73

N

NAFTA, 92

National Longshoremen's Board (NLB), 50–51

Nickels, Greg, 43

Nickelsville, 43

Nintendo Co., Ltd., 89

Nippon Yusen Kaisha, 16, 92

Nisqually earthquake, 98

Nissan Line, 80

Normandy Park, 91

North American Free Trade Agreement (NAFTA), 92

Northern Pacific Railroad, 14–15

Northwest Airlines, 53, 64–65. *See also* Northwest Orient Airlines

Northwest Cruise Ship Association, 101

Northwest Orient Airlines, 87

Northwest Passage, 108

Norwegian Cruise Line, 98

Norwegian Star, 98

O

Olympia, 13, 32, 79

Opheim, J. Eldon, 73, 116

Oregon Territory, 12, 32

Oregon Trail, 12, 32

P

Pacific Coast Company, 36

Pacific Maritime Association, 101

Pacific Rim, 85, 99

Pacific Steamship Company Terminal, 52

Paetzke, Dick, 99

Paine Field, 53

Panama Canal, 10, 22, 24, 28, 35, 88, 104, 108

Pan-Atlantic Steamship Corporation, 71

Panic of 1893, 21

Pier 16, 75

Pier 17, 75

Pier 20, 75

Pier 28, 66

Pier 30, 66

Pier 36, 52

Pier 37, 52

Pier 38, 52

Pier 39, 52

Pier 40, 50, 51

Pier 41, 32, 50, 51

Pier 42, 52, 71

Pier 43, 59

Pier 45, 59

Pier 48, 59

Pier 49, 59

Pier 57, 79

Pier 64, 86, 94–95

Pier 65, 86, 94–95

Pier 66, 51, 52, 86, 94–95, 97

Pier 69, 94, 113

Pier 70, 44

Pier 86 Grain Terminal, 79–80, 82

Pier 90, 32, 33, 57, 81

Pier 91, 32, 33, 57, 81, 82, 107

Pier A, 32

Pier B, 32

Piner's Point, 11, 12

Pioneer Square, 11

Populist Party, 21, 23, 24, 25, 34, 36

Port District Act, 17, 23, 24–25, 27–28

Port of Shanghai, 89

Port of Tacoma, 52, 53, 80, 88, 93

Port Townsend, 17

Portage Bay, 22

Portland, 16

Post Alley, 9, 11, 15

Princess Cruises, 32, 100, 101

Progressive Movement, 20, 21, 36

Puget Sound, 10, 12, 13, 14, 15, 17, 22, 29, 31, 32, 34, 48, 58, 79, 82, 88, 101, 104, 108

Q

Queen Anne, 27, 32, 79, 94, 113

R

Railroad Avenue, 9, 10, 11, 15–16, 17, 20, 21, 24, 43, 44, 94

Rainier Brewery, 42

Remsberg, Charles E., 24, 25, 29, 37–38, 115

Roosevelt, Franklin D., 50, 52, 55

Roslyn Coal & Coke Company, 94

Rowe, Gordon, 61, 115

Roy, Donald Francis, 43

Royal Caribbean International, 32, 98

S

Salmon Bay, 22, 27, 29, 31, 58, 59, 75

Samish Bay, 13

Scott, Tyree, 74

Sea-Land Industries, 71, 73, 88

Seattle Chamber of Commerce, 25, 28, 30, 59, 93

Seattle City Light, 101

Seattle Coal and Fuel Company, 11

Seattle Commercial Club, 24–25

Seattle General Construction Co., 75

Seattle Longshoremen's Co-Operative, 36

Seattle Municipal League, 25, 35, 61

Seattle Port Commission, 21, 25, 28–30, 34–35, 36, 37–38, 45–46, 58, 60–61, 66, 67, 69, 90, 94, 95, 102, 107, 112, 116

Seattle Post-Intelligencer, 22, 28, 30, 45

Seattle Times, The, 22, 24, 28, 30

Seattle–Tacoma International Airport, 52, 53, 55, 60, 64–65, 74, 76–79, 83, 87, 88, 90–93, 95, 97, 98, 100, 102, 103–104, 108–109, 113

Seattle-Tacoma Shipbuilding Corporation, 51

Selassie, Haile, 61

Semple, Eugene, 75

Shilshole Bay Marina, 66, 73, 112, 113

Simpson Timber Company, 42

Skid Road, 43

Skinner & Eddy, 37, 43

Smith Cove Cruise Terminal, 32-33, 107

Smith Cove Park, 112

Smith Cove, 11, 16, 27, 29, 30, 31, 32–33, 35, 38, 39, 43, 51–52, 57, 81, 109, 113

Smith Tower, 115

Smith, Charles L., 46

Smith, Henry A., 32

Smith's Cove, 32

Smoot-Hawley Tariff Act, 44

Sound Transit Central Link, 108

Space Needle, 75

Stevedores, Longshoremen, and Riggers Union (SLRU), 48

supersonic transport (SST), 76

T

T-91 Bike Trail, 94

Taft-Hartley Act, 57

Terminal 5, 66, 73, 75, 80, 90, 93, 100, 103, 112

Terminal 10, 75

Terminal 18, 75, 90, 105

Terminal 25, 80–81, 90

Terminal 28, 80–81, 108

Terminal 30, 75, 81, 90, 100, 107

Terminal 37, 4, 81

Terminal 42, 90

Terminal 46, 42, 43, 52, 59, 79, 90, 109

Terminal 86, 79, 80, 81, 92, 101, 104, 113

Terminal 91, 11, 32, 50, 81, 82, 92, 93, 94, 107, 112

Terminal 102, 75

Terminal 103, 75

Terminal 104, 75

Terminal 106, 75, 89

Terminal 107, 43, 75, 116

Terminal 108, 75,

Terminal 115, 75, 77, 80

Terminal 117, 102

Territorial Legislature, 32

The Boeing Company. *See* Boeing Company, The

Thompson, Cappy, 88

Thomson, Reginald H., 20, 21, 23, 24

Totem Ocean Trailer Express (TOTE), 80

Trade Development Alliance of Greater Seattle, 93

Treadwell, George T., 64, 116

Truman, Harry, 57

Tukwila, 66, 91, 108

Tulalip Indian Reservation, 32

Tumwater, 17

U

U.S. Army Corps of Engineers, 22, 102

U.S. Fish and Wildlife Service, 102

U.S. Maritime Commission, 60

United Air Lines, 53, 87

United Express, 90

USS *Decatur*, 12

V

Vietnam War, 82, 87

Villard, Henry, 14

W

Washington Chemical Works, 31

Washington Emergency Relief Administration, 43

Washington State Grange, 35

Washington State Legislature, 20, 21, 24, 35, 51, 69, 79

Washington Territory, 12, 14

Waterfront Employers Association (WEA), 38, 45, 46

Waterfront Employers Union, 38

Watson, Steve S., 50

West Waterway, 66, 73, 75

Western Airlines, 60, 64–65

Western Avenue, 9, 10, 11, 15

Western Washington, 10, 34

Weyerhaeuser, 42, 86, 99

Wilkes Expedition, 12

World Trade Center, 97

World Trade Organization, 97, 99

World War I, 7, 35, 36, 38, 43, 48, 51, 75, 87

World War II, 5, 32, 43, 52, 57, 64, 70, 75, 87

Y

Yesler Way, 12, 30

Yesler, Henry, 11, 12, 17, 43

Yesler's Mill, 11, 12, 32, 43

Yesler's Wharf, 11, 12–13, 17, 43

Yoshitani, Tay, 43, 102, 103–104, 116